KAMA SUTRA

THE ANCIENT ART OF MAKING LOVE
FOR THE NEW MILLENNIUM

Author
Madelyn Carol Dervos
Publisher
Attar Incorporated
Westlake Village, California

Editors: Evelyn Vuko, Rob Love
Design: Rob Love
Calligraphy: Eva Lynn
Lotus Design: Denise Puchbauer

Copyright © 1998 by Attar Incorporated
Copyright © 2000 by Attar Incorporated
Copyright © 2002 by Attar Incorporated
Copyright © 2003 by Attar Incorporated
All rights reserved

Attar Incorporated
755 Lakefield Road, Suite J
Westlake Village, CA 91361
phone: 805-496-9525
fax: 805-496-0275
website: www.kamasutra-thebook.com
Library of Congress catalogue card number 00-110762
ISBN 0-9668398-1-1
Printed in U.S.A.

To: _____

From: _____

Message: _____

_____

_____

_____

_____

_____

_____

"This work is not to be used merely as an instrument for satisfying our desires. A person acquainted with the true principles of this science, who preserves his Dharma (virtue or religious merit), his Artha (worldly wealth) and his Kama (pleasure or sensual gratification), and who has regard to the customs of the people is sure to obtain the mastery over his senses. In short, an intelligent and knowing person attending to Dharma and Artha and also to Kama, without becoming the slave of his passions, will obtain success in everything that he may do."

VATSYAYANA

About This Book

*I*n this age where the representation of lovemaking has often become so raw, and the time to linger in the arms of those we adore so challenged by the frantic lives we lead, Vatsyayana offers some sanity. He reminds us that this ancient act of making love is an art that requires sensitivity and an open sense of adventure. He talks of the care and preparation that can be made when a lover is expected. He discusses methods for preparing our home, a room, our bed to receive and honor that special person. He teaches that lovemaking can be a profound expression of appreciation toward the person who inspires an unexplainable and beautiful feeling; a feeling that wells up deep from within—a feeling that comes when it comes, that stays for as long as it stays, and leaves when it leaves, if it leaves.

Little is known about Vatsyayana. It is believed that he was a religious scholar and that the Kama Sutra he wrote was based on a collection of ancient works written by authors, many of whom have been lost in the mists of time.

The original Kama Sutra is far more than a sex manual. It offers a perspective on the art of making love that is often lost in the West. One of the great works of ancient Indian literature, Vatsyayana's Kama Sutra offered the people of his time a complete approach to one of their pillars of life; KAMA, the principal of love, pleasure and sensual gratification. Although a variety of similar works have been produced over the ages in India, Vatsyayana's work is regarded as the definitive reference in the West.

Life for the Indian citizens of Vatsyayana's time, and indeed today, is believed to be founded on; DHARMA, the acquisition of religious merit; ARTHA, the acquisition of wealth and property; and KAMA, love, pleasure and sensual gratification. It is believed, if all three are practiced successfully in this life, they lead to MOKSHA, the ultimate liberation of the soul from the cycle of rebirth.

The first acknowledged translation of the Kama Sutra from the ancient Sanskrit into English was by Sir Richard Burton in 1883, and that work has become the basis for contemporary versions of the Kama Sutra. Burton's efforts were first published only as a limited edition in England. Many other versions have appeared, but most are really only vehicles for various individual's interpretation of love making. As a result, they bear little relationship to Vatsyayana's expression.

This book is not an attempt to recreate Vatsyayana's India. What he observed applied to a time and a culture that is now mostly of historical interest. The scholastic language Burton used more than a century ago has not only crossed the Atlantic, but has also changed over time. What we are offering is the essence of Vatsyayana, edited according to the language and culture of this age.

While it's true Vatsyayana compiled his seven parts some time around the 1st to 6th centuries, he returns us to the special moods of mystery and spirituality that can be appreciated by people of any age and era joining in love. ❧

Sir Richard Burton

*T*hose of us who are about to enjoy this great work of Indian literature should pause perhaps for a few moments and give silent thanks to the members of the Kama Shastra Society of Benares and London—all two of them!

Sir Richard Burton, explorer, linguist and author, and Foster Fitzgerald Arbuthnot, a retired Indian civil servant, met when they were both relatively young. Arbuthnot was 20 and Burton 32. The younger man was considered amiable, quiet, determined and to hold liberal views on marriage. Burton, however, evoked a much stronger reaction. He was described by writer Arthur Symons as "gypsy in his terrible magnetic eyes—the sullen eyes of a stinging serpent. His face has no actual beauty in it; it reveals a tremendous animalism, an air of repressed ferocity, a devilish fascination."

Burton struck Wilfred Blunt in a similar way when they met. "He reminded me by turns of a black leopard, caged but unforgiving. . . . In his talk he effected an extreme brutality and, if one could have believed the whole of what he said, he had indulged in every vice and committed every crime." But at the same time, Blunt observed that Burton's intimidating appearance "gave place at times to more agreeable expressions.". . . Therefore, Blunt understood "the infatuated fancy of his wife and that in spite of his ugliness he was the most beautiful man alive."

Despite the apparent differences in character, both Arbuthnot and Burton shared a common passion—India. Arbuthnot was to live there almost his entire life. In 1842, Burton became an ensign in the Indian army in Bombay and was to later throw himself into studying most of the major Indian languages. Aided by two of his tutors, he began moving around Indian society in disguise. Burton even went so far as to buy three shops in Karachi. He came to know Indian life intimately.

Some years later, after personally exploring Indian sexual values and practices in great detail he translated the Kama Sutra. The Kama Shastra Society privately published Sir Richard Burton's translation in 1883. The thick paper, vellum bound edition was distributed among a select group of friends. It was so popular that there was a second reprint two years later.

A third "silent" associate of the Kama Shastra Society duo was Richard Monckton Milnes. Burton was very moved by his friendship with this man, who was to become Lord Houghton. He wrote in the preface of his third volume of the Arabian Nights that Milnes had "during a friendship of 26 years shown me the most unwearied kindness." Milnes had been the Society's patron and it was his lusty appetite for erotica that kept Burton in pursuit of knowledge about sex.

The Kama Shastra Society was to publish many exotic works translated by Burton, including his massive 16 volume translation of the Arabian nights. More than 1,000 copies were produced, which realized a small fortune for Burton.

But just five short years after the second edition of the Kama Sutra was published, Burton died and, with his passing, the Kama Shastra Society also vanished. Burton's legacy was the opening of an extraordinary window into exotic literature. The name Kama Sutra has become an icon of erotica. Had it not been for Burton's passion, a work revered in India and produced by Vatsyayana all those centuries ago might never have been discovered by the west. ❧

CONTENTS

PART EIGHT: THE ILLUSTRATED POSITIONS

Kama is the process of using the mind and the soul
in the enjoyment of the five senses—
hearing, feeling, seeing, tasting and smelling.

The main ingredient is the contact
between the organ of sense and its object.

Being aware of the pleasure
that comes from that contact
is called Kama.

And it is Kama that can be learned
from the Kama Sutra.

PART ONE

LOVE PRINCIPLES

Dharma, Artha and Kama

"Man, the period of whose life is one hundred years, should practice Dharma, Artha and Kama at different times and in such a manner that they may harmonize together."
Vatsyayana

*V*atsyayana spends a little time discussing the principles of Dharma and Artha, but to fully appreciate these subjects requires an understanding of Indian culture or the willingness to read extensively.

Briefly, Dharma is obedience to the command of the Shastra or Holy Writ of the Hindus and should be learned, Vatsyayana believes, from those who understand it.

Artha is the acquiring of arts, land, wealth, vehicles, equipment and friends. Added to that is the protection of what is acquired and the increase of what is protected. Artha should be learnt from those versed in the ways of commerce.

Kama is the process of using the mind and the soul in the enjoyment of the five senses—hearing, feeling, seeing, tasting and smelling. The main ingredient is the contact between the organ of sense and its object. Being aware of the pleasure that comes from that contact is called Kama. And it is Kama that can be learned from the Kama Sutra.

A man who employs the many
arts and sciences of the Kama Sutra
will reach his objectives and enjoy a fine woman.

Such a man is looked upon with love by his own wife,
and by women in general.

Chapter *Two*

The Arts and Sciences to be Studied

"Man should study the Kama Sutra and the arts and sciences subordinate thereto, in addition to the study of the arts and sciences contained in Dharma and Artha. Even young maids should study the Kama Sutra along with its arts and sciences before marriage, and after." Vatsyayana

A woman should learn the Kama Sutra, at least in part, with some confidential friend. They should study in private. Her teacher might be one of the following people: a trusted girlfriend, an aunt, an old family friend, or her own sister. A young woman should study the arts and sciences of the Kama Sutra both before and after marriage. What follows are the suggested arts to be studied:

The Art of Personal Adornment

> Applying perfumed ointments to the body.
> Dressing the hair with oils and perfumes, and braiding it.
> Preparing perfumes and scents.
> Coloring, dyeing, staining garments, hair, nails and bodies.
> Henna tattooing and design.
> Stringing necklaces, garlands and wreaths.
> Weaving flowers into the hair.
> Making earrings, jewelry and decorations for dresses.
> Making costumes for masquerades and holiday parties.

The Arts of Interior Design and Handicrafts

> Arranging beds of flowers and spreading flowers on the ground.
> Making artificial flowers.
> Making stained glass lamps and windows.
> Making mosaic picture frames, mirror frames, tabletops or walls and floors.

Making beds comfortable and inviting.
Spreading out soft carpets and floor pillows.
Picture making, trimming and decorating.
Changing the appearance of things; refinishing yard sale furniture to look like antiques, painting wood or walls to look like marble.
Pottery and sculpture in clay.

The Home Arts

Cooking and developing recipes.
Knowledge of nutrition and a variety of healthy diets.
Making lemonades, sherbets and flavored drinks. Making and designing clothes, curtains, tablecloths, pillows and bed linens.
Fancy handwork like needlepoint, embroidery, crocheting, knitting.

The Physical and Social Arts

A woman and man might attract each other by singing, playing musical instruments and dancing, or by a combination of all three.
Planning, designing and preparing parties for birthdays, surprises, anniversaries, graduations, holidays and religious and occasions.
Playing cards, board games, games of chance, and doing jigsaw puzzles.
Playing tennis, squash, hiking, rock climbing, boating, swimming, volleyball, yoga, aerobics and martial arts.
Learning the rules of society, paying compliments and respecting each other.
Knowing how to read the character of a man from his features, speech and body language.

The Art of Verbal Play and Writing

Learning how to mimic, imitate and create fictitious characters for the amusement of your lover.
Reading aloud, including novels, poetry and letters.
Inventing terms of endearment and nicknames in a variety of languages.
Learning, speaking and writing foreign languages.
Learning regional slang and expressions. Composing poetry, writing love letters and cards.

Carpentry and wood working.
An appreciation of houses and their design.
Knowledge of jewelry and precious stones.
Growing ornamental or edible plants and gardening.
Economics of personal and household finance.

Why should a woman learn these arts? Even the bare knowledge of them makes a woman attractive. She can easily support herself by acquiring these talents, whether she has a husband or not. Vatsyayana adds that "a man who is versed in these arts gains very soon the hearts of women." ❧

The citizen should avoid
any societies that are disliked,
lawless or destructive.

He should live in a society
that abides by the will of the people
and has pleasure as its objective.

Such societies are highly respected
in this world.

Chapter Three

The Life of the Citizen

"Having thus acquired learning, a man, with the wealth that he may have gained by gift, conquest, purchase, deposit or inheritance from his ancestors, should become a householder and pass the life of the citizen." Vatsyayana

A man should buy or rent a home in a popular city or large town, in a good neighborhood. It could be located near water, and contain a variety of rooms. Ideally, it should be surrounded by a garden with an arbor, a swing and comfortable places to sit.

Inside, one of the rooms should be scented with rich perfumes and contain a canopy bed that is soft, covered with clean white linens and scattered with flowers. It should have at least two pillows, one at the top and another at the bottom. Place a comfortable couch and table close by. On the table, put fragrant body oils, colognes and flowers, as well as containers of eye drops, mouthwash and lemon slices for perfuming the mouth. On the floor near the bed, keep favorite books, trinkets and hobby materials like musical instruments or paper and pencils for sketching. In the same room, arrange a small table and chairs conveniently for games and hobbies. Enhance the atmosphere by placing cages of singing birds outside the room.

The life of the citizen is enhanced by keeping his body desirable. He should bathe, brush his teeth and shave daily, applying lotions, deodorants, ointments and cologne sparingly. After doing these things each morning, he should dress with appropriate clothes and jewelry, and check his appearance in a mirror. He should then eat things that freshen the mouth and breath, and begin his day. Meals should be taken morning, afternoon and night. After breakfast, time should be devoted to caring for and training animals and pets. After lunch, a nap is recommended. The afternoons are best spent in the company of friends. Evenings are set aside for a favorite woman to whom the citizen is attached. In the special room he has prepared, the woman should be welcomed and entertained with loving and agreeable conversation. So ends the duties of the day.

For diversion or amusement, the following things can be done occasionally: attend festivals and celebrations or parties and picnics where both men and women can gather and share refreshments.

Festivals

On special public and religious holidays, the citizen and his friends can host performances of singers and musicians. Hospitality and payment, perhaps even prizes, should be provided to the performers.

Social Gatherings

When the citizen and his friends get together with women, in his home or another's, they should compose poetry or test each other's knowledge in various arts.

Drinking Parties

Men and women should drink in each other's houses. Drinks can be either with or without alcohol. If beer, wine and liquor are being served, the attributes of each beverage can be discussed. For example, micro brewing, imported beers verses local varieties, vineyards, vintages and the types of wines.

Going to Gardens or Picnics

On summer afternoons, the citizen and his friends can go on picnics and swim together in safe, clean rivers, lake, pools or the ocean. They can go horseback riding through parks and fields. After these pleasant diversions, they should return home, bringing bunches of flowers.

Other Social Diversions

Evenings can be spent playing games of chance or going out for walks on moonlit nights. Celebrating spring. Picking fruits and vegetables. Finding and eating edible flowers. Eating the tender ears of corn. Picnicking in the forests when the trees are budding. Water sports. Decorating each other with flowers. Pelting each other with flowers. Attending local and regional festivals and celebrations. These and other similar amusements should always be done by the citizen.

A respected professor, a personal instructor, or a trusted friend with a sense of humor should be employed to help the citizen solve his quarrels with women. A citizen should visit all the neighbors in his community. He should mingle at social gatherings. He should gratify his friends with his presence by helping them and encouraging them to help each other. The citizen should be acquainted with foreign languages, local slang and dialect. He should avoid any societies that are disliked, lawless, or destructive. He should live in a society that abides by the will of the people and has pleasure as its objective. Such societies are highly respected in this world. ⚘

Chapter Four

Types of Women—Friends—Messengers

"The object of practicing Kama with other women (other than one's wife) is neither enjoined nor prohibited. The object of practicing Kama with such women is pleasure only." Vatsyayana

The types of women a man has a sexual relationships with can be varied: single women, divorced women, or prostitutes. The woman might even still be married to another man. On such occasions, the man should be aware of the woman's desires, and the moral and religious values of his society.

A man might have a relationship because he has an objective in mind. It could be to create an alliance against an enemy, master a difficult situation, or pave the way to attain greater wealth and/or social position.

For example, a relationship with a married woman should be for a special reason, not just sexual pleasure. Such relationships can be dangerous, however, especially if the woman wants a relationship and the man does not.

The following women should be avoided:

Those with a contagious disease
A woman with psychiatric problems
One who can't keep a secret
A woman who is blatant about her desire for sexual relations
Women who smell bad
A cousin
A female friend
A woman who leads a life of austerity
The wife of a relative or friend

The following are the kind of friends a citizen can turn to:

Those from childhood
One who has an obligation to him
One who shares the same disposition and taste
A classmate
A confidante
A friend of the family

These friends should possess the following qualities:

They should tell the truth
Their nature shouldn't change over time
They should agree with your plans
They should stand firm, not be envious or disloyal
They should keep your secrets

Friendships should be formed with people of many different socioeconomic, religious and cultural backgrounds.

A person carrying a message for the citizen should be skillful and bold. The messenger should be able to interpret a response accurately. He or she should have good manners and a sense of propriety. He or she should be ingenious in business, fast to comprehend and able to remedy a situation quickly.

A man who is creative and sensible, who has a sense of decorum, who can read the intentions of others who and has good friends can very easily win over the most challenging of women. ❦

A man who is creative and sensible,
who has a sense of decorum,
who can read the intentions of others
and has good friends,
can very easily win over
the most challenging of women.

PART TWO

INTERCOURSE

Chapter One

Sexual Union According to Size, Passion and Time

"There are, then, nine kinds of union according to dimensions. Amongst all these, equal unions are the best." Vatsyayana

Before discussing the kinds of union, or intercourse, Vatsyayana divides people into categories to the size of their sexual organs. Using symbols from the animal kingdom, he classifies men with the smallest penis as the hare, those larger as the bull, or largest, as the horse.

Women are divided into three classes based on the depth of their vaginal tract. Again using animal symbols, women range from shallow, the female deer, to the mare, to the deepest, which he labels the female elephant. Though these labels are graphic and perhaps not always complimentary, corresponding size should be considered for the sake of comfort and sexual gratification of both lovers.

Equal

Men	Women
Hare	Deer
Bull	Mare
Horse	Elephant

Unequal

Men	Women
Hare	Mare
Hare	Elephant
Bull	Deer
Bull	Elephant
Horse	Deer
Horse	Mare

Based on corresponding dimensions then, there are three equal unions: the hare and the deer, the bull and the mare, the horse and the elephant. There are six unequal unions, or unions when the physical dimensions don't correspond: hare and mare, hare and elephant, bull and deer, bull and elephant, horse and deer, horse and mare.

Particularly for men, the horse and the mare, the bull and the deer form what Vatsyayana calls "high union", but the horse and the deer form the "highest." For woman, the elephant and the bull, the mare and the hare form "low unions", but the elephant and the hare form the "lowest". Simply put, the largest and smallest combinations in size of either sex organ is the worst.

The force of passion or desire is a crucial element in sexual intercourse. Vatsyayana ranks nine kinds of intercourse based on small, middling or intense amount of sexual desire. A man whose desire for sex is not great, whose semen is scanty and who can't bear the embraces of a woman is called a man of "small" passion. Men with stronger feelings are men of "middling" passion. Those full of passion are labeled "intense". Women also have three degrees of feeling as illustrated below:

Men	*Women*
Small	Small
Middling	Middling
Intense	Intense

Men	*Women*
Small	Middling
Small	Intense
Middling	Small
Middling	Intense
Intense	Small
Intense	Middling

According to the length of time in love-making, there are three kinds of men and women: short-timed, moderate-timed and long-timed. In combination, this makes for nine different kinds of sexual intercourse.

16

A woman's timing is often determined by her lover. If a man is long-timed, she might love him more. If he is short-timed, she might not be able to be satisfied by him. Some women can easily be satisfied, others take a long time to reach orgasm. A man should be aware of the natural rhythms of the woman's passion and play to its weaknesses and strengths.

If the man's passion is intense during his first lovemaking session with a woman, his timing is short; but this can be improved by continued lovemaking. If the woman's passion is weak during her first lovemaking session with a man and her timing is long, her passion can be quickened by continued lovemaking.

Vatsyayana believes that though a man's body and a woman's body be different and their timing not be equal, the pleasure they derive from lovemaking can be the same. This pleasure comes naturally from the acts of lovemaking that each performs. Based on the size of sexual organs and the degrees of passion and time, uncounted kinds of lovemaking can be produced. In each particular kind of sexual union, men and women should use such means as they think are suitable for the occasion.

On the different Kinds of Love

Love is of four kinds:

> Love acquired by continual habit
> Love resulting from the imagination
> Love resulting from belief
> Love resulting from the appreciation of external objects

Sometimes love results from continually practicing a habit like sexual intercourse, hunting, fishing, drinking, or gambling. Love can happen merely from imagining and dwelling on ideas such as thinking about kissing and embracing a loved one. Love can come when two people feel it mutually, experience the truth of it and consider each other to be their very own. Love can blossom from appreciating and enjoying external things and objects, like houses, cars, art, music.

What has been said in this chapter about sexual union is only a beginning. In the following chapters it will be treated at length and in detail. ✾

آیات وتفاوت ساحوال آیات هراینه دلالتها بست روشن و جهدار كافندرت اللقوم

يعقلون مردیم كه نقل كمند تلك آیات الله این دلالتها بعد رت ای این

آیتها غونشتلوها علیك مجوام بربا الجوت مربانی درستی وبای حدیث

Chapter Two

The Embrace

"Even those embraces not mentioned in the Kama Shastra should be practiced at the time of sexual enjoyment, if they are in any way conducive to the increase of love and passion." Vatsyayana

There are four kinds of embraces which indicate the mutual love of a man and woman:

Touching
Piercing
Rubbing
Pressing

The following types take place only when a woman and man don't yet know each other:

Touching embrace:
when a man goes in front or alongside a woman and touches her body with his own.

Piercing embrace:
when a woman bends down as if to pick up something and "pierces" a man with her breast, and the man in turn takes hold of them.

The following types are for those who already know each other's intentions:

Rubbing embrace:
when walking slowly together, two lovers rub their bodies against each other.

Pressing embrace:
when one of the lovers presses the other forcibly against a wall or pillar.

When meeting, the following four kinds of embraces are used:

The twining of a creeper
Climbing a tree
Mixing sesame seeds with rice
The milk and water embrace

These two kinds of embraces take place when the lovers are standing:

The twining of the creeper:
a woman clinging around a man, bends his head to hers with the intention of kissing him. She makes soft sounds with her teeth and lips.

Climbing a tree:
a woman places one of her feet on the foot of her lover, the other on one of his thighs, one arm around his neck and the other around his back. She makes soft singing and cooing sounds as she attempts to "climb up him" for a kiss.

These two kinds of embrace take place when the lovers are lying down and having intercourse:

Mixing sesame seeds with rice:
the lovers lie so closely that their arms and legs are entwined and rubbing against each other's.

Mixture of milk and water:
when a man and a woman are very much in love with each other and they embrace each other as if they were entering into each other's bodies. This can be done with the woman sitting in the man's lap or in front of him.

Embracing body parts:

> The embrace of the thighs
> The embrace of the lower part of the body, from the navel to the thighs
> The embrace of the breasts
> The embrace of the forehead

Embrace of the thighs:
when one of two lovers presses forcibly one or both of the thighs of the other

between his or her own.

Embrace of the lower body:
when a man presses the woman's body against his own and mounts her to tickle, nibble, pat or kiss.

Embrace of the breasts:
when a man places his breast between the breasts of the woman and presses her with it.

Embrace of the forehead:
when either lover touches the mouth, the eyes and the forehead of the other with his or her own.

Any kind of embrace can be done at the time of sexual enjoyment, particularly if it increases the love or passion. When passion is rising, Vatsyayana believes the rules of the Kama Sutra should be applied. However, once the wheel of love is set in motion, there are no rules and no order. ❧

Once lovers become
familiar with each other,
moderation is not necessary.

Chapter Three

*K*issing

"Anything may take place at any time, for love does not care for time or order."
Vatsyayana

*T*here is no certain time or order between an embrace, a kiss, fondling and caressing, but that all these things should generally be done before intercourse. When a couple makes love for the first time, all these things should be done moderately, alternately and for not too long.

Once lovers become familiar with each other, moderation is not necessary. They can continue for as long as they like. Or they can do all things at once, especially when they want to kindle love.

Places for kissing:
the forehead, eyes, cheeks, throat, chest, breasts, lips and the interior of the mouth. The joints of the thighs, the arms and the navel may be kissed as well.

There are three sorts of kisses, particularly when a woman is young:

> The nominal kiss
> The throbbing kiss
> The touching kiss

The nominal kiss:
when a woman only touches the mouth of her lover with her own, but does not return his kiss.

The throbbing kiss:
when a woman touches the lip that is pressed into her mouth and moves her lower lip, but not the upper one.

The touching kiss:
when a woman shuts her eyes, places her hands on those of her lover and touches her lover's lip with her tongue.

There are other kinds of kisses:

> The straight kiss
> The bent kiss
> The turned kiss
> The pressed kiss
> The greatly pressed kiss
> Kiss of the upper lip
> Clasping kiss
> Fighting of the tongue

Straight kiss:
when the lips of two lovers are brought into direct contact with each other.

Bent kiss:
the heads of the two lovers are bent towards each other.

Turned kiss:
one of them turns up the face of the other by holding the head and chin.

Pressed kiss:
the lower lip is pressed with force.

Greatly pressed kiss:
the lower lip is held between two fingers, touching it with the tongue, then pressing it with great force with the lip.

Kiss of the upper lip:
the man kisses the upper lip of the woman while she kisses his lower lip.

24

Clasping kiss:

one lover takes both the lips of the other between his or her own. A woman should only accept this kind of kiss from a man who has no mustache.

Fighting of the tongue:

touching the teeth, the tongue and the palate of the lover with the tongue.

There are different kinds of kisses, based on their meaning or intention. When a woman looks at the face of her lover while he is asleep and kisses it to show her desire, it is called a "kiss that kindles love." A kiss that is given to distract a lover's attention from a quarrel or when he is looking at something else, is called a "kiss that turns away." When a man arrives home late at night and kisses his sleeping woman to show her his desire, it is called a "kiss that awakens."

Kissing the reflection of a loved one in a mirror, in water, or on a wall, is called a "kiss showing the intention." When a person kisses a child or a picture, or an image, or a figure in the presence of their lover, it is called a "transferred kiss." If a man kisses the finger of a woman's hand in a public place, like a movie theater, or if he kisses a toe while she's sitting, it is called a "demonstrative kiss." A woman gives a "demonstrative" kiss when she is lathering a man's body in a bath or shower and places her face on his thigh or toe, and kisses him to inflame his passion.

Kissing games

Making bets as to who will get kissed first.
Kissing a sleeping lover and holding the lower lip between the teeth.
Pinching, tickling, scratching, nibbling or nipping with the teeth, especially when there is intense passion.

Kissing is further categorized by the amount of pressure on the lips:
Moderate, contracted, pressed and soft

Different kinds of kisses are appropriate for different parts of the body. In fact, whatever things done by one lover to another should always be returned. A kiss should always beget a kiss. ❀

Chapter Four

Pressing, Marking, and Scratching with the Fingernails

"But pressing with the nails is not a usual thing except with those who are intensely passionate. It is employed, together with biting, by those to whom the practice is agreeable." Vatsyayana

When love becomes intense, pressing with the fingernails or scratching can happen between couples who find it pleasant and stimulating. It can happen the first time lovers are together, or in the excitement of leaving or returning from a trip together. Pressing or scratching can be used to reconcile an angry lover or when one of the lovers is intoxicated.

Pressing with the nails leaves eight types of marks:

> Sounding
> Half moon
> A circle
> A line
> A tiger's nail or claw
> A peacock's foot
> The jump of a hare
> The leaf of a blue lotus

Sounding:
softly, audibly scratching the chin, breasts, lower lip, or the pubic area with the nails, making the lover's hair stand on end. This type of pressing can be used when a lover shampoos the other's hair, scratches the head, or merely teases and bedevils.

Half moon:
the curved mark of the nails impressed on the neck and the breasts.

27

Circle:
half moons pressed opposite each other. This mark is generally made on the navel, small hollows on the buttocks and on the joints of the thigh.

Line:
a mark in the form of a small line made on any part of the body.

Tiger's Nail:
a small curved line made on the breast.

Peacock's Foot:
a curved mark on the breast made by the five nails. Since this mark requires great skill to make properly, it should be praised.

Jump of the Hare:
five marks of the nails made close together near the nipple.

Leaf of the Blue Lotus:
a mark made on the breast or hips in the form of a leaf of the blue lotus flower.

The places that are to be pressed with the nails are as follows: the armpit, throat, breasts, lips, pubic area, middle parts of the body and the thighs. When passion makes a lover impetuous, the places need not be considered.

The qualities of good nails are that they should be bright, well set, clean, entire, convex, soft and glossy in appearance. Nails are of three kinds, according to their size:

Small
Medium
Large

Large nails give grace to the hands and, on men, are said to attract women. Small nails can be used in various ways, and applied only to give pleasure. Medium nails have the properties of both.

When a lover leaves on a journey and makes a mark of three or four lines close to one another on the thighs or breast of the lover, it is called "a token of remembrance." This one is especially recommended for husbands to give to their wives, to increase their love.

Love is renewed when a lover sees the marks of nails on the private parts of his or her body, even if the marks are old and almost worn away. If there are no marks of nails to remind a person of the passages of love, then love is lessened. Nothing tends to increase love so much as the effects of marking with the nails and biting.

There are uncounted ways of making marks with the nails. Vatsyayana says variety is necessary in love, so love is to be produced by means of variety. ❧

If men and women act according
to each other's nature and liking,
their love for each other will not fade,
even in one hundred years.

Chapter Five

Biting

"All the places that can be kissed are also the places that can be bitten, except the upper lip, the interior of the mouth and the eyes." Vatsyayana

Good teeth are bright, in proper proportion, unbroken and have sharp ends. Bad teeth are blunt, protruding, rough, soft, large or loosely set.

There are different types of biting:

> The hidden bite
> The swollen bite
> The point
> The line of points
> The coral and the jewel
> The line of jewels
> The broken cloud
> The biting of the boar

Hidden bite:
shown only by the excessive redness of the skin that is bitten. Done on the lower lip.

Swollen bite:
the skin is pressed down on both sides. Done on the lower lip or left cheek.

Point:
a small portion of the skin is bitten with two teeth only. Done on the lower lip.

Line of points:
small portions of the skin bitten with all the teeth. Love marks for the forehead, throat, armpit, thighs and joints of the thighs.

The coral and the jewel:
done by bringing together the teeth and the lips. The lip is the coral, the teeth the jewel. Done on the left cheek.

Line of jewels:
biting with all the teeth. For the throat, armpit, joints of the thighs.

The following two types of bites are done by intensely passionate people:

Broken cloud:
raised marks in a circle coming from the spaces between the teeth. Done on the breasts.

Biting of the boar:
broad rows of marks near one another, with red intervals between them. Done on the breasts and shoulders.

Kissing, pressing with the nails and biting are all love ornaments placed on the left cheek. Marking with the nails or biting the earrings or corsage of a woman are signs of desire.

In lovemaking, men should only do things that are agreeable to women and suit their nature. Some women are naturally proud and reserved, and won't welcome nail marks or biting. Some welcome all types of unusual pleasures, like being slapped or spanked. There are women who love strong language during love-making, others don't. Some women prefer being discreet about their sexual nature. There are women who, though rubbed and pressed during the sex act, are slow to lubricate and orgasm. Others lubricate richly and orgasm quickly, sometimes numerous times. Some women prefer to cover their bodies during sex and others despise. Some love oral sex or making special sounds during the act of love. There are those with soft bodies who speak sweet words of love.

Those things that increase passion, like kissing and embracing, should be done first. Those done only for amusement or variety should take place afterwards.

When a man bites a woman forcibly, she should bite him back doubly hard. A "point" should be returned with "a line of points"; a "line of points" should be returned with "a broken cloud". If a woman is excessively bitten, she has good cause to begin a lovers quarrel. Begin by holding the lover by his hair, bend his head down and kiss him on the lower lip. Then closing your eyes, bite him in various places.

If a man shows a woman love marks she gave him in public and in broad daylight, she should smile and show him the marks he gave her. If men and women act according to each other's nature and liking, their love for each other will not fade, even in one hundred years. ❧

Different kinds of intercourse
performed to the liking of each individual
generates love, friendship and respect
in the hearts of women.

Positions

"An ingenious person should multiply the kinds of congress after the fashion of the different kinds of beasts and of birds." Vatsyayana

When deer-woman, a woman with a small, shallow vagina, has intercourse with bull-man, a man with a large penis, she should lie down in such a way as to widen her vaginal opening. When elephant-woman, a woman with a large, deep vagina, makes love with hare-man, a man with a small penis, she should lie down in a way that contracts her vagina. This is also true of mare-woman, a woman of medium size. When people with same size sexual organs make love they can lie down in any natural position. When a large-sized woman makes love to a small-sized man, she should make use of any lotions or medicines that quicken her desire.

The Deer-woman has the following three ways of lying down:

> The widely opened position
> The yawning position
> The position of the wife of Indra

The widely opened position:
lowering her head and raising her middle. Lubricants make penetration easier in this position.

The yawning position:
raising her thighs and keeping them wide apart.

The position of the wife of Indra:
bending her legs against the sides of her body. This position takes practice and is useful when the size of the man is much larger than the woman.

The clasping, pressing, twining and mare's position that follow, are best used when a woman makes love to a man whose penis is smaller than her vagina.

The clasping position:
the legs of both the woman and man are stretched out straight. This can be done on the side or flat on the back. In the side position, the man should lie on his left side, the woman on her right. This rule should be observed in lying down with all kinds of women.

The pressing position:
after the clasping position has been started, the woman presses her lover with her thighs.

The twining position:
the woman places one of her thighs across the thigh of her lover.

The mare's position:
the woman holds the man's penis in her vagina. This is only learned through practice.

There are many other ways of lying down when making love:

Rising position:
the woman raises both of her thighs straight up.

Yawning position:
the woman raises both of her legs and places them on her lover's shoulders.

Pressed position:
when the man grabs both of the woman's legs and holds them against his chest. When one leg is stretched out, it is called the "half pressed position."

Splitting of the bamboo:
the woman places one of her legs on her lover's shoulder, and stretches the other out and continues on, alternating her legs.

Fixing of a nail:
the woman places her leg on the man's head and the other is stretched out. This position is only learned by practice.

The crab's position:
both of the woman's legs are bent and placed on her stomach.

Packed position:
the thighs are raised and placed one on top of the other.

Lotus-like position:
the calves are placed one on top of the other.

Turning position:
while penetrating the woman, the man turns his body around and the woman embraces his back. This is only learned by practice.

Supported intercourse:
a man and a woman support themselves on each other's bodies, or on a wall, or pillar while standing.

Suspended intercourse:
the man stands against a wall, places his hands under the woman and raises her up. She throws her arms around his neck, puts her thighs on either side of his waist and moves herself with her feet against the wall.

Congress of a cow:
a woman crouches over like a cow and the man mounts her like a bull. At this time, everything that is ordinarily done chest to chest is now done on the back. Characteristics of different animals can be imitated during intercourse like a dog, goat, deer, donkey, cat, tiger, elephant, boar or a horse.

When a man enjoys two women at the same time, both of whom love him equally, it is called the "united congress." When a man enjoys many women altogether, it is called the "congress of a herd of cows." Intercourse can happen in the water or while mimicking the play of mating animals, such as a bull elephant with a group of female elephants, a herd of goats or deer.

Many young men can enjoy a woman who is the wife of one of them either one after the other or at the same time. One of them can hold her while another has intercourse with her, a third one uses her mouth, a fourth holds her middle so that they enjoy different parts of her alternately.

Anal intercourse can also be done and is called "lower congress."

Different kinds of intercourse, performed to the liking of each individual, generates love, friendship and respect in the hearts of women. ❀

Women Acting the Man's Part; The Work of the Man

"When a woman sees that her lover is fatigued by constant congress without having his desire satisfied, she should, with his permission, lay him down upon his back and give him assistance by acting his part." Vatsyayana

A woman may also reverse roles to satisfy her lover's curiosity or her own desire. There are two ways of doing this during intercourse. First, when a woman turns around and gets on the top of her lover, or secondly when she plays the role of the man from the beginning. She should let her hair down, smile, breathe hard and press her breasts against her lover's. Lowering her head frequently, she should also say, "I was laid down by you and worn out with lovemaking. Now I shall lay you down in return."

The work of the man is whatever is done to give pleasure to the woman. For example, while the woman is lying on his bed distracted by conversation, he should loosen her undergarments and, if she objects, overwhelm her with kisses. When his penis is erect, he should touch her with his hands and manipulate various parts of her body. If the woman is shy and if this is their first lovemaking session, the man should place his hands between her thighs which probably are kept close together. If she is a very young girl, he should first place his hands on breasts, under her armpits and on her neck. If she is a sexually-experienced woman, he should do whatever is agreeable or fitting for the occasion. After this he should take hold of her hair and hold her chin in his fingers, and kiss her. The man should gather from the action of the woman what things would be pleasing to her during intercourse. While a man is doing what he likes best, he should make a point of pressing those parts of a woman's body that she indicates with a look.

Signs of sexual enjoyment and satisfaction in women are when the woman's body relaxes and she closes her eyes. She loses all shyness and shows her willingness to bring their sexual organs as close together as possible.

Signs that a woman is not sexually satisfied are when she shakes her hands, she does not let the man get up, feels dejected, bites him, kicks him and continues moving after he has finished. In such cases the man should rub the woman's vagina with his fingers until he feels a softening. Then he should penetrate her with his penis.

The acts to be done by the man are:

> Moving forward
> Friction or churning
> Piercing
> Rubbing
> Pressing
> Giving a blow
> Blow of the boar
> Blow of the bull
> The sporting of a sparrow

Moving forward:
the organs are brought together directly.

Friction or churning:
the penis is held in the hand and turned around inside the woman's vagina.

Piercing:
lowering the woman's hips and piercing the upper part of her vagina with the penis. Rubbing is the same thing done on the lower part of the vagina.

Pressing:
the vagina is pressed by the penis for a long time.

Giving a blow:
the penis is removed to some distance from the vagina and then forcibly strikes it. When only one part of the vagina is rubbed this way, it is called the "blow of the boar." When both sides are rubbed, it is called "the blow of the bull"

Sporting of the sparrow:
when the penis is moved up and down frequently inside the vagina without being taken out.

When a woman reverses roles with a man, she can do the following things in addition to the nine just mentioned:

The pair of tongs
The top
The swing

The pair of tongs:
holding, drawing in and pressing the penis in the vagina for a long time.

The top:
when a woman turns around like a wheel while having intercourse. This takes practice.

The swing:
the man lifts up the middle part of his body and the woman rotates her middle part.

When the woman is tired she should place her forehead on her lover's and rest without separating the organs from each other. After her rest, the man should begin lovemaking again.

If the woman is reserved and keeps her feelings concealed, she shows all her love and desire when she gets on top of a man. A man should learn from the actions of the woman what her disposition is, and in what way she likes to be enjoyed. Menstruating women, women who have recently given birth and very heavy women should not be made to reverse roles with the man. ❧

Oral Sex

"A bird is clean when it causes a fruit to fall from a tree by pecking at it . . . . And the mouth of the woman is clean for kissing and such like things at the time of sexual intercourse." Vatsyayana

*T*he following are eight things a woman can do with her mouth on a man's penis:

The nominal congress
Biting the sides
Pressing outside
Pressing inside
Kissing
Rubbing
Sucking a mango fruit
Swallowing up

Nominal congress:
holding the man's penis with her hand, and placing it between her lips and moving it around her mouth.

Biting the sides:
covering the end of the penis with her fingers collected together like the bud of a tulip, and pressing the sides of the penis with her lips and teeth.

Outside pressing:
pressing the end of the penis with the lips closed and kissing it as if drawing it out.

Inside pressing:
putting the penis far into the mouth, pressing it with the lips and then taking it out.

Kissing:
holding the penis in her hand, the woman kisses it as if kissing the lower lip.

Rubbing:
after kissing, touching the tongue all over the penis and passing the tongue over the end of it.

Sucking a mango fruit:
putting the penis half-way into the mouth and forcibly kissing and sucking it.

Swallowing up:
the woman puts the whole penis into her mouth, and presses it to the very end, as if she were going to swallow it up.

Kissing a woman's vagina should also be learned because it is different from kissing the mouth. When a man and woman lie down with the head of the one towards the feet of the other, it is called the "congress of a crow".

A man should take note of the place, time and practices he carries out. He should determine what he does or doesn't like. Since these things are done privately, no one knows what any person will do at any particular time and for what purpose. Vatsyayana thinks that in all these things connected with love, everybody should act according to their own customs and inclinations. ❧

Chapter   *Nine*

Beginning and Ending Intercourse;
Circumstances of Love Making; Love Quarrels

"A man skilled in the sixty-four arts is looked upon with love by his own wife, the wives of others and by courtesans." Vatsyayana

*I*n a pleasant room, maybe decorated with flowers and fragrant with perfumes, the citizen should invite a woman to eat and drink. The woman herself should be freshly bathed and dressed. The citizen should then seat the woman on his left side, stroke her hair and clothing and embrace her with his right arm. They should then carry on an amusing conversation about various subjects. They may also talk suggestively of coarse things not generally mentioned in refined society. They may then sing, play music, talk about the arts and persuade each other to drink. In time, the woman may be overcome with desire. This is often the beginning of sexual union.

After love making, the lovers, with modesty, should wash up. After this, the man might massage the woman with lotions and creams. He should then embrace her with his left arm and with comforting words, hold a cup of water for her to drink. Then they can eat soups, hot cereals, fruits, juices, sweets, or sherbets; anything sweet, soft and pure.

The lovers may also sit on the terrace and enjoy the moonlight, and chat. While the woman lies in his lap, the citizen can show her the different planets, the morning star, the polar star, the Great Bear.

Lovemaking can be of the following kinds:

Loving
Subsequent love
Artificial love

Transferred love
Spontaneous love

Loving:

when a man and a woman who are in love come together after a difficult moment. Or when one of the two returns from a journey, or they reconcile after a quarrel. Loving is done according to the couples liking, and for as long as they choose.

Subsequent love:

two people come together while their love for each other is still in its infancy.

Artificial love:

when a man excites himself by any of the means discussed in previous chapters. Or when a man and woman attached to different people come together. At this time all the ways and means mentioned in the Kama Sutra should be used.

Transferred love:

when a man makes love to one woman while thinking of another.

Spontaneous love:

lovemaking that takes place between two people who are attached to one another. Done in anyway that is pleasing to them.

Love quarrels

a woman who is very much in love with a man cannot bear the mention of or conversation about a rival. Nor can she bear being called by her rival's name by mistake. If this happens, a quarrel can occur. The woman might cry, become angry, even strike her lover.

The man should attempt to reconcile her with soothing words and by placing her carefully on the bed. She might pull his hair, kick him and then head for the door. She should sit near the door but not leave, as this might go against her. If the man continues with conciliatory words and actions, she should then embrace him. She should rebuke him for his mistakes while showing him a desire for lovemaking.

When the woman has quarreled with her lover, she should go to him, express her anger and then leave. At this time, the citizen should bring in a respected, trusted friend with a sense of humor to help him solve his quarrel. If the argument is resolved, the woman should spend the night with her lover.

A man who employs the many arts and sciences of the Kama Sutra will reach his objectives and enjoy a fine woman. Such a man is looked upon with love by his own wife and by women in general. These arts are also dear to women; they add to their talents, heighten their charm and increase the respect they receive. ❀

PART THREE

ACQUIRING A WIFE

Chapter One

Marriage

"When a girl of the same caste, and a virgin, is married in accordance with the precepts of Holy Writ, the results of such a union are the acquisition of Dharma and Artha, off-spring, affinity, increase of friends and untarnished love."

Vatsyayana

*V*atsyayana believes a man should attach himself to a woman from a good family, whose parents are alive, and who is three or more years younger than himself. Her family should be respected, wealthy, well connected, and have many relatives and friends. She should be beautiful, healthy and have a good disposition. She should have good hair, teeth, ears, eyes and breasts. The man should, of course, also possess similar qualities. True love transcends age, family traits and personal appearance. Some believe that prosperity can only be attained by marrying the one you love.

To encourage a marriage, the parents, relations and friends should assist. Friends might inform the woman's parents of the faults of any other man who wants to marry her. They could exaggerate the qualities and family background of their friend to endear him to the parents, especially the mother. They should mention any good omens and signs they perceive about this union.

A man should marry when all the signs seem right. He should not marry a sleepy, tearful woman or one who runs at the thought of marriage. He should not marry a woman who is engaged to another.

Vatsyayana says the following should also be avoided:

A woman with an odd name
One whose nose is flattened or the nostril turned up
One who is built like a man
One who is bent over

One whose legs are bowed
One who has a prominent forehead
One who is bald
One who has been diseased by another
One who has swollen glands
One who is disfigured in any way
A friend
One whose hands and feet continually perspire

When a woman is of marriageable age, her parents should dress her well and display her for all to see. They should encourage her to accompany her friends to sports and wedding ceremonies. They should show her to advantage out in society because she is a precious commodity. Kind words and signs of friendship from perspective suitors and their families should be welcomed. Dates should be encouraged, even arranged. In good time, the families involved should dine together and encourage the marriage.

When a man and woman become engaged they should marry according to their desires and customs. The best connection is made between equals; partners who are mutually pleasing and families who respect each other. A man should never marry a woman to whom he feels superior or inferior, nor should he feel that way about her family. This is also true for a woman. ❧

Chapter Two

Creating Confidence in the Woman

"For the first three days after marriage, the woman and her husband should sleep on the floor, abstain from sexual pleasures, and eat their food without seasoning it either with alkalis or salt." Vatsyayana

For the next week, they should bathe, listen to music, dress up, dine together, and entertain relatives and friends who come to wish them well. During this time, the man should use soft words to create confidence in his wife. He should avoid sudden or forcible approaches to love making. Women want tender beginnings.

The man should approach the woman in ways that please her and build her confidence. He should embrace her first of all in a way she likes most. Embraces of the upper part of the body are easier and simpler, and can be done by candle-light, moonlight or in darkness. If she is unwilling to embrace, he should kneel at her feet. It is a universal rule that, however modest or angry a woman may be, she never disregards a man kneeling at her feet. He should then kiss her mouth softly and gracefully, making no sound. When he has gained her respect, he should encourage her to talk by asking her questions about herself. He should ask about their relationship; about her desire and feelings for him. A woman who doesn't converse easily with her man may be encouraged by a mutual female friend.

Once the wife is familiar with the husband, she should place ointments, creams and lotions near their favorite place for making love. The man should begin lovemaking by gently pressing his fingernails against her breasts and embrace her, passing his hand repeatedly over and around her body. He should draw her into his lap, make love ornaments on her body with his lips and nails, and gently tease her like a child.

After the woman's confidence has increased further, he should feel her whole body with his hands and kiss her all over. He might even wash her body, especially the thighs. After reaching this point, he should touch her private parts, loosen her dress and, lifting it up, shampoo the joints of her naked thighs. If the woman is particularly reluctant or shy, lovemaking should not begin just yet.

The married couple might then begin to learn the arts and sciences of the Kama Sutra together. The man should tell her how much he loves her and describe the hopes he had about her before he married her. He should dispel all her fears of rivals.

A man should try to win a woman's affection so that she will love him and place her confidence in him. This is not done simply by following the woman's inclinations or by opposing her wishes. A man should adopt a middle ground with a woman. A man who knows how to make a woman love, honor and respect him creates confidence in her and wins her over. When a man neglects a woman because she is modest or shy, he is ignorant of the working of the female mind. It is even possible that a woman may come to despise a man who does not understand her nature. A man who forces himself on a woman does not understand the heart of a woman and makes her feel nervous, uneasy, dejected and hateful toward the man who took advantage of her. When her love is not understood or returned, a woman becomes despondent, hates her husband and might turn to other men. ❦

Chapter   *Three*

Courtship and Displaying Feelings

"A poor man possessed of good qualities, a man born of a low family possessed of mediocre qualities, a neighbor possessed of wealth, or one under the control of his father, mother or brothers, should not marry without endeavoring to gain over the girl from her childhood to love and esteem him." Vatsyayana

When a man begins to court the woman he loves, he should spend time with her. He should amuse her with games and diversions that suit their age and the stage of their relationship. They might pick and collect flowers and make garlands. They might cook together, play games or cards, or work out in a gym together. They might amuse themselves with friends.

The man should make an effort to meet a woman's friends and show them great kindness. By doing so, they won't interfere with his intentions, and perhaps even encourage his relationship with the woman.

The man should do whatever the woman takes most delight in, and he should get for her whatever she desires. He should get her curious and unusual gifts: like exotic dolls made of cloth, wood, or porcelain; or gifts for cooking; or figures in wood like a man and woman standing together or pairs of rams, goats, or sheep. He might give her gifts that symbolize ancient gods or goddesses, bird cages, vases and bottles in elegant forms, musical instruments, picture frames, perfumes, or cosmetics. Such things should be given at different times; some should be given in private, others in public. In short, the man should try in every way to make the woman look to him as one who would do everything for her.

When her love begins to show signs of increasing, he might tell her entertaining stories. He might delight her with magic tricks or juggling. If she shows curiosity about a particular form of art, like drawing, he should show her his own skill. If she is delighted by singing, he should entertain her with music. On certain special days, they should attend affairs and festivals. After she returns

53

from a trip, he should greet her with flowers or jewelry for the head, ears or fingers.

The man should find subtle, indirect ways to let the woman know that he is familiar with the Kama Sutra. Under this pretext, he should also inform her of his great skill in the art of sexual enjoyment.

While courting a woman, a man should wear his finest clothes and make as good an appearance as possible. Women love men who are clean, good looking, well dressed and amusing.

It is not true that women make no effort to win over the man they love. A woman can show her love by a variety of outward signs and actions.

She might tantalize a man by not looking him directly in the eye or crossing her legs to show her thighs. She might tease him by answering with murmurs or incomplete sentences. If he is across the room, she might attract his attention by laughing or talking in a peculiar tone. She might draw his attention to her by pointing out different things. She might keep him by her side for a longer period of time by very slowly telling him tales and stories. She might pull a child on her lap, and kiss and hug it. She might move gracefully or athletically while he's watching. She might confide in his friends. She might encourage a friend to take a love token, like a flower, to him. She avoids being seen by her lover when she is not dressed and made up. She should always wear any gift he might have given her.

When a man perceives that a woman has feelings for him, he should do everything in his power to bring them together. He should win her over with teasing games, artful skill and with the help of her confidential friends. ❦

Chapter Four

Winning the Woman; Winning the Man

"When engaged with her in any game or sport, he should intentionally hold her hand." Vatsyayana

When a woman begins to show her love as described in the previous chapter, the man should try to win her over in the following ways:

He should practice the various embraces, such as the touching embrace. He should draw her attention to couples portrayed in paintings or sculpture. When swimming in a pool together, he should dive in far away and emerge close to her. He should show an increased liking for all the budding signs of spring. He should describe the pangs he suffers on her account. He should tell her about his dreams. At parties and gatherings, he should sit near her and touch her under some pretense or another, placing his foot on hers and slowly touching her toes, pressing the ends of the toenails. He might take her foot in his hand and do the same thing. Whenever he gives anything to her or takes anything from her, he should show her by his manner and look how much he loves her.

When alone with her in a lonely place, or in darkness, he should make love to her and tell her the true state of his mind without distressing her in any way.

Whenever he sits with her on the same seat or bed he should say to her, "I have something to tell you in private." When she comes near, he should express his love to her more by manner than by words. When he comes to know her feelings, he should pretend to be sick so she will come to him and take care of him. He should hold her hand and place it on his eyes and head, and tell her she is the only one who can make him better. He should let her leave whenever she wants to, with a passionate request to come and see him again. This "illness" should be continued for three days and three nights during which she might get into the habit of seeing him more frequently. Then he should carry on long conversations with her, because a man never succeeds in winning over a woman without a great deal of talking.

When a woman makes her feelings obvious, the man can then begin to be alone with her and enjoy her. As for those who say that women's desires for lovemaking are strongest in darkness or in the evenings, this is only idle talk. Women, when approached at proper times and in proper places, do not turn away from their lovers.

Some say that, although a woman loves a man very much, it is not dignified to make the first overtures toward him. However, when the man makes it known that he is interested, she should respond favorably but demurely when he embraces her. She should receive all his outward shows of affection as if she were ignorant of his state of mind. When he tries to kiss her, she should oppose him. When he begs for lovemaking, she should let him fondle her intimately only with a struggle and not give in to his demands. When she is certain she is truly loved, and that the man is devoted to her and will not change his mind, she should then relent and persuade him to marry her quickly. After a woman loses her virginity, she should tell her confidential friends about it.

A woman who is highly sought after should marry the man she likes; one who will be obedient to her and capable of giving her pleasure. A woman who marries to please others never becomes attached to the man. A man who is obedient to a woman yet master of himself is better than one who has had many relationships with women.

A man who is small minded, disgraceful or travels too frequently does not deserve to be married. Nor does one who is devoted to sports and gambling, and only to comes to his wife when he likes. Of all the lovers of a woman, a true husband possesses qualities she likes. Such a husband deserves honor and respect because he is the husband of love. ❧

Chapter Five

Certain Forms of Marriage

"When the girl is gained over and acts openly with the man as his wife, he should cause fire to be brought from the house of a Brahman, because it is the opinion of ancient authors that a marriage solemnly contracted in the presence of fire cannot afterwards be set aside." Vatsyayana

When a woman cannot make up her mind or isn't ready to marry, the man might convince her if he has the help of one of her trusted female friends, or her brother or sister. He should convince them of his great love for her, and perhaps even present them with gifts. Whether the woman he loves is gardening or visiting friends, he should press his cause. If she is spending the night with him, he might even awaken her gently and talk of his desire to make her his wife.

A man and woman should marry according to their own religious and cultural customs. Marriages thrive when they are made in favorable circumstances and respect the desires of both the man and the woman. The fruit of all good marriages is love. ❧

PART FOUR

ABOUT A WIFE

Chapter One

The Way a Virtuous Woman Lives

"A virtuous woman who has affection for her husband should act in conformity with his wishes, as if he were a divine being, and with his consent should take upon herself the whole care of his family." Vatsyayana

A woman should maintain a clean home and arrange flowers throughout its rooms. The floors should be smooth and polished or carpeted, giving the living areas a neat appearance. A garden should surround the house or, in an apartment, greenery and plants can grace window boxes or balconies. In the garden she might plant green vegetables, fruit trees and herbs like mustard, parsley and fennel. She might cultivate jasmine, roses or fragrant grasses. The garden should have a well, pool or tank in the middle. Depending on the season, she might plant radishes, potatoes, beets, mangoes, cucumbers, eggplant, pumpkins and squash, garlic and onion. A wife who takes pride in her home attracts the heart of her husband.

In meal preparation, she should use healthy, nutritious foods that appeal to their particular tastes and needs. The kitchen should be clean and located in a quiet place of the house.

When accompanying her husband, the wife should dress attractively and wear her jewelry. She should neither extend or accept invitations without first consulting her husband. She should not involve herself in sports or games that could cause friction between them.

In the event of misconduct on the part of her husband, the wife should not blame him excessively. She should rebuke him with conciliatory, not abusive words, whether he is alone or in company. She should never be a scold. She should avoid bad expressions, sulky looks and making comments on the side. She should not stare at strangers or remain in lonely places for too long. Her body, her teeth and her hair should be tidy, sweet and clean.

In the evening, during private times with her husband, the wife should wear colorful clothing, jewelry, flowers, and apply sweet-smelling perfumes, lotions and powders. During the daytime, her clothing can be of plainer materials and she can wear just a touch of scent.

The wife should shop when items are on sale. Perfumes, ointments, salves and medicines should be kept in stock and stored in convenient places. The amount of money she spends should depend on the amount of money earned each year. She should make use of left-overs and prepare some foods like bread at home when possible. She might sew. She should stock up on cleaning supplies, hardware and household goods. If she employs people to help with cleaning and gardening, she should be responsible for paying them, as well as paying for car repair or pet care. She should be kind to those people and reward them on holidays. She should give old clothing and household goods to those who will appreciate them. She should take care of all sales and purchases for the household.

The wife should not tell strangers about family finances, or tell family secrets. She should strive to be more clever, attractive, proud, a better cook and much more attentive to her husband than other women. She should not be vain or consumed with her own pleasures.

She should welcome and entertain her husband's friends in the home. Towards the parents, relations and friends of her husband, the wife should behave as they deserve. She should avoid the company of undesirable people.

When her husband is away on business or traveling, the woman should maintain her best appearance. Though anxious to hear about her husband, she should still maintain the normal household routines and attend to any repairs. She should not spend long periods of time visiting her friends or relatives. She should not overspend. When her husband returns, she should greet him attractively dressed and perhaps with a gift.

The wife who leads a good life, and is devoted to her husband and family will enhance their standard of living and keep her husband devoted to her. ❧

The Conduct of a Wife

"The causes of re-marrying during the lifetime of the wife are as follows: The folly or ill-temper of the wife, her husband's dislike to her, the want of offspring, the continual birth of daughters, the incontinence of the husband." Vatsyayana

From the beginning of the marriage, a wife should try to attract the heart of her husband by being devoted, good tempered and wise.

A young woman should not marry a man whose poor character will one day force her to leave him or seek another man. A widow should marry again if happiness can be found in another man. She should marry the person of her choice and one who will suit her. Happiness is secured by marrying a man who possesses good qualities and loves enjoyment.

When a widow remarries, either she or her new husband can pay for the parties, picnics and gifts for the relatives and friends. The couple can mutually exchange wedding gifts. If, however, she chooses to leave him, she should return all the gifts except those mutually exchanged. If he leaves her, she should not return anything at all.

After her marriage, she should live in her husband's house. She should demonstrate that she is well versed in the arts and sciences of the Kama Sutra. She should treat all his family members with kindness; the people who work in and around the house with generosity, and all his friends with good temper.

In quarrels with her husband, she should not rebuke him, but in private make use of the Kama Sutra for enjoyment. She should treat children of friends with gifts and make toys for them. She should enjoy parties, picnics, fairs, festivals, and all kinds of games and amusements.

When a woman feels her husband dislikes her, she might get back in his good graces using the following ways:

By being a good nurse to their children
By showing his friends her devotion to him
By leading their children in their spiritual duties
By not holding too high an opinion of herself
By making peace when family members quarrel
By encouraging reconciliation between quarreling members
By being aware of her husband's weak points, but keeping them secret
By behaving in such a way that her husband can't help but see her devotion

To please a husband, a wife might:

Bring him flowers
Bring him lotions, creams or colognes
Buy him new clothes

A man should act fairly toward his wife. He should not disregard or pass over her faults, but gently chide her. He should not speak of anyone who is a rival for his affections. He should confide in her, respect her, flatter her, buy her gifts and honor her with his lovemaking. A woman who has a good temper, and a strong spiritual and moral sense, wins her husband's devotion and vanquishes all her rivals. 🪷

PART FIVE

ABOUT THE WIVES
OF OTHER PEOPLE

The Characteristics of Men and Women

"The wives of other people may be resorted to but the danger to oneself when uniting with them should first of all be examined." Vatsyayana

A man may turn to another man's wife when his love for her becomes so increasingly powerful that he begins to suffer. This intensity increases by degree and progresses in the following order:

1. Love of the eye
2. Attachment of the mind
3. Constant reflection
4. Destruction of sleep
5. Emaciation of the body
6. Turning away from objects of enjoyment
7. Removal of shame
8. Madness
9. Fainting
10. Death

Women should be judged, not by outward appearances, but by their conduct, how they express their thoughts, and by their body language.

Though a woman might fall in love with every handsome man she sees and a man with every beautiful woman, they don't always take the next step for a variety of reasons. In love, certain things are often particular to women. A woman generally loves without regard to right or wrong and not for any particular gain. A woman might shrink from a man's first advances though she may be interested in him. However, if his attempts are consistent, she might then become convinced.

What is morally right or wise can often stop a man's feelings for a woman despite her attempts to win him over. Sometimes, when a man fails to win over a woman, he will just give up and walk away. There are times, too, when a man will win a woman and then become indifferent to her. It is not true, however, that a man does not care for what is easily won and only desires what he cannot have.

There are many causes why a married woman will reject another man's advances:

Affection for her husband

The man is inaccessible

Anger at being addressed by the man too familiarly

The man travels too much to be sure of his intentions

He might be attached to another woman

Fear that the man might not keep his feelings a secret

Feeling that the man is obsessed by his friends

Fear that he is not passionate

Concern about his being in too powerful a position, such as an employer

Fear of him being fickle

Fear of him being forceful

Fear of him being too clever

Fear that his passion is impetuous

He is a friend

He lacks worldly wisdom

He has poor character

Disgust at his blindness to her love for him

His passion is weak

Conflicting sizes of sexual organs

Concern that his passion jeopardizes his well being

Despair over her own imperfections

Fear of discovery

Disillusionment over his age or appearance

Fear that he may be conspiring with her husband

He is too moral

A man should try to remove these impediments from the very beginning. If the woman is hesitant because the man is in a powerful position, he should reassure her by demonstrating his great love and affection. If he is not accessible to her, he should make himself familiar and available. Lack of character can be overcome with wisdom and acts of bravery. Neglect is mended by extra attention. Fear can be conquered with proper encouragement.

The following men are generally successful with women:

> Experts in the science of love
> Skilled story tellers
> Childhood friends
> Confidants
> Generous with gifts
> Well-spoken
> Men who do things a woman likes
> Men who have not loved another woman before
> Men who act as messengers
> Men who acknowledge their weaknesses
> Friends of a woman's female friends
> Men who are close with their female friends
> Good looking men
> Men who have been brought up with women
> Men who are desired by good women
> Neighbors
> Men who love sexual pleasures
> Recently married men
> Sociable men
> Liberal men
> Strong men, like Bull men
> Enterprising and brave men
> Men who are better looking, better educated and more liberal than the woman's husband
> Men who dress well and live magnificently

The following women are easily won over:

> Women who are always out and available
> A woman who is always staring at a man
> A female messenger
> A woman who looks sideways at a man
> A woman who hates her husband, or who is hated by him

A woman who has nobody to care for her or supervise her
A sociable woman
A woman who makes a show of being affectionate with her husband
A widow
A poor woman
A woman fond of sex
The wife of a man with many younger brothers
A vain woman
A woman whose husband is inferior to her in ability
A woman disturbed by her husband's misdeeds
A woman who has outgrown the man she married
A woman who is ignored by her husband
A woman whose husband travels too much
A jealous woman
A lazy woman
A coward

Natural desire is strengthened and secured when enhanced by art and wisdom. Men can be successful with women by carefully observing them and overcoming their doubts. ❧

Chapter *Two*

Meeting a Woman

"When they do meet, the man should be careful to look at her in such a way as to cause the state of his mind to be made known to her. He should pull about his mustache, make a sound with his nails, cause his own ornaments to tinkle, bite his lower lip and make various other signs of that description." Vatsyayana

A man should make the acquaintance of the woman he loves in the following way:

He should make arrangements to be seen by the woman casually or by creating a special opportunity. A casual meeting might be when he visits her home or she comes to his. A special opportunity is one arranged by a friend or one that occurs at public occasions like weddings, festivals or parties.

When they finally do meet, the man should look at the woman in such a way that his intentions are obvious. In her company, he should speak to his friends about her, displaying an easy, open, sociable nature. He should ignore the attentions of other women or act bored when they speak to him. While she is listening, he can hold a conversation full of double meanings with a child or some other person in which he makes his feelings known for her. In her company, he should make gestures and demonstrations of his affection for her like carving their initials in a tree or writing her name in the sand. If she is sitting with a child on her lap, he should play with the child, using it to stimulate conversation with her. If the woman still lives at home with her parents, he should make himself known to them and use his relationship with them as an excuse to visit. While visiting them, he should talk lovingly about their daughter, making sure she overhears.

As his intimacy with her increases, he should give her some of his things to keep for him, like his favorite cologne or cigars. In order to see her frequently, he should arrange to use the same vendors she does, like her grocery store, jeweler, bank, laundry. He might pay her long visits under the pretext of doing business with her.

Whenever she wants anything, or if she is in need of money, or wishes to acquire a skill, he should help her to the best of his ability. He should hold discussions with her in the company of other people. They should discuss things together like business, hobbies, books, movies, sports, music, art, poetry. He should introduce her to new things and discuss their value. He should make a point of telling her that he agrees with her in every way.

When a woman makes it known by outward signs that she loves the man, the man should make every effort to win her. Young women with little or no sexual experience should be treated with the greatest delicacy and considerable caution. When the woman's intentions are known and her shyness put aside, the couple can begin to exchange simple or valuable gifts. He might give her a sweet smelling flower or put one that she'd been wearing in his buttonhole.

He should dispel her fear and hesitation, take her to a quiet place and kiss and embrace her. After giving her a gift, he should embrace her, press her and caress her private parts.

When a man is trying to seduce one woman, he should not attempt to seduce another at the same time. A wise man would not think of seducing a woman who is apprehensive, timid, untrustworthy or too sheltered by her family. ❦

Chapter   *Three*

A Woman's State of Mind

"A woman who lets a man make up to her, but does not give herself up, even after a long time, should be considered as a trifler in love. But, owing to the fickleness of the human mind, even such a woman can be conquered by always keeping up a close acquaintance with her." Vatsyayana

When a man is trying to win a woman, he should make a point of understanding her state of mind. If she does not seem interested, he should ask his friends to help him convince her. If she meets him once, then comes to meet him better dressed than before, or in a private place, he should be encouraged. When a woman avoids a man because she has too much respect for him and has pride in herself, she might be won over if he keeps a favorable relationship going or enlists the help of a clever friend.

When a man approaches a woman and she reproaches him with harsh words, she should be avoided. When a woman reproaches a man yet acts affectionately, she should be made love to in every way. A woman who meets a man in lonely places and puts up with the touch of his foot, but pretends to ignore it, can be won over with patience and effort.

If she falls asleep near him, he should put his left arm around her and gauge her reactions when she awakens and finds it there. She might want him to repeat it. He can also do this with his foot. If he succeeds this time, he can embrace her more closely. If she stands up and moves away from his embrace, but behaves with him as usual the next day, she may still be interested in him. If, however, she does not appear again, he might then enlist the help of a convincing friend.

When a woman gives a man an opening, and makes her own love obvious, he should enjoy her. The signs of a woman showing her love are:

She calls out to a man before he calls out to her

She displays herself to him in secret places
She trembles and mumbles when she speaks to him
Her face and hands perspire, her face blooms with delight
She offers to wash his back or shampoo his head
She shampoos with one hand and touches with the other
She washes his thighs
She makes excuses to touch him when he is motionless

Lastly, when she has resisted all his efforts to win her over, she returns the next day to shampoo his body again

When a woman neither encourages or discourages a man but remains aloof, he might ask a convincing friend to intervene for him. If she still shows no encouraging signs, the man should think long and hard before making any further attempts.

A man should arrange to get himself introduced to a woman, and then carry on a conversation with her. He should hint at his attraction for her. If she responds favorably, he should proceed without fear. A woman who responds the first time can be easily won over. Some intensely passionate women can be won over in a moment. Whether women be wise, simple or confiding, those who openly show their love are easily won. ❧

Chapter Four

A Go-Between

"If a woman has manifested her love or desire, either by signs or by motions of the body, and is afterwards rarely or never seen anywhere, or if a woman is met for the first time, the man should get a go-between to approach her." Vatsyayana

The intervention of a trusted friend in the dynamics of a new relationship can be helpful to a couple. A confidante can make a man's rivals seem a poor choice in the eyes of the desired woman. He can praise her beauty, wisdom, generosity and good nature, telling her that only his friend is fit to love her. This trusted friend can reiterate the faults of other suitors, their jealousy, ingratitude, anti-social behaviors, meanness, dullness, lack of passion. He should stress his friend's suffering on account of his inability to establish a relationship with her. The man's friend should describe his friend's talents, skills in the sensual pleasures, his compatibility, and even embellish the truth.

This friend should carefully note any favorable changes in the woman's response. He should sensitively inquire about her health, her activities, her hobbies, her family. He should ask about her last encounter with his friend and then, with laughter and encouragement, cast it in the best light.

The best person to intervene on a man's behalf is a friend the woman knows and has confided in, but has not shown that person any signs of affection.

This friend might even bring the woman a gift from his friend. Gifts of flowers, perfume, jewelry or love letters are appropriate. The best gifts illustrate the man's thoughtfulness or speak to the woman's tastes. If she loves white violets, his gift should be white violets. The gift should cause a woman to return a gift to the man. Then, a meeting between the lovers should be set up by the friend.

This meeting should be at a public place like a party, the movies, the theater, at a wedding or festival. A suitable place would also be the home of a female friend. Whatever the place, it should provide comfortable entry and exit for both people.

When a woman intervenes on behalf of a woman friend, she can take over all the above-mentioned tasks or just a part of them. She might only deliver a letter when the couple can't frequently meet. She might act without her friend's knowledge. When a woman takes over all the tasks to bring two lovers together, she usually knows both persons. She might be sent by either one. She might bring two friends together whom she believes are well-suited but have never met. By clever conversation, she might bring a woman together with a man whom her friend had not thought of before. Or she might approach someone her friend considered beyond her aspirations. She might even reunite people who have been separated.

A woman who goes to a man herself and tells him of having had a sexual dream about him intervenes for herself. The man should meet such a woman privately.

The danger of sending a friend to intervene is that the friend might end up the winner of the person desired. ❧

Chapter Five

People in Authority

"Persons in authority should not do any improper act in public, as such are impossible from their position and would be deserving of censure." Vatsyayana

Should a man in a high position require sexual pleasures with a woman other than his wife, he might send a friend to intervene on his behalf. He might meet a married woman who will respond to his desires in a store he frequents, or she might be someone who works for him like his hairdresser, housekeeper, lawyer or doctor. He might meet women at sporting events or parties. He might invite a woman to his place of work for a party or ceremony. He might ask a female friend to give her a tour of his home or gardens, and inform the woman of his interest in her. Should the woman refuse, she should be given some small gift to show that there are no hard feelings.

A wise man who is in a position of power should keep the welfare of the people in his heart and not put any of these methods into practice. A man who has conquered lust, anger, greed, spiritual ignorance, pride and envy can become powerful among people. ❧

A clever man is never deceived by his own wife.

A man should never seduce another man's wife
because it can destroy
his material and spiritual wealth.

This book should be used to teach men
ways to guard and protect their own wives
not to seduce the wives of others.

Chapter Six

The Keeping of One's Own Wife

"A man should not cause his innocent wife to be corrupted by bringing her into the company of a deceitful woman." Vatsyayana

A man should protect his wife's reputation. A woman's reputation can be destroyed in the following ways:

She shows no restraint
She goes out too often alone
By the loose habits of her husband
A lack of caution in her relations with other men
The continued or long absences of her husband
Living in a foreign or unknown country
Destruction of her love and feelings by her husband
The company of woman who are free with their sexual favors
The jealousy of her husband

A clever man is never deceived by his own wife. A man should never seduce another man's wife because it can destroy his material and spiritual wealth. This book should be used to teach men ways to guard and protect their own wives, not to seduce the wives of others.

PART SIX

ABOUT COURTESANS

Introductory Remarks

*V*atsyayana used a treatise about courtesans written almost two thousand years ago as the basis for the next six chapters. Sir Richard Burton, the original translator, notes that although a great deal has been written about the courtesan, nowhere is there a better description of her, her belongings, her ideas and the workings of her mind, than in the Kama Sutra.

The Hindus have always had the good sense to recognize courtesans as a part of human society and, so long as they behaved with decency and propriety, they were regarded with a certain respect. In fact, because courtesans were both educated and amusing, they were far more acceptable companions than most married or unmarried women. Courtesans in the eastern cultures have rarely been treated with the brutality and contempt so common in the Western world.

Some women in all levels of society are said to be born courtesans and follow their instincts. However, it has also been said that every woman naturally has an inkling of the profession and does her best to make herself agreeable to men.

In the following pages, the subtlety of women, their wonderful perceptive powers, their knowledge, and their intuitive appreciation of men and all things are illustrated in great detail. Even women today can learn from the ways of the ancient courtesan. ✤

Chapter One

Attracting the Right Kind of Man

"By having intercourse with men, courtesans obtain sexual pleasure as well as their own maintenance." Vatsyayana

When a courtesan is inspired by love, her action is natural. When she is with a man solely to make money, her action is artificial. She should, however, conduct herself as if her love is natural because men place confidence in women who apparently love them. In making her love known to the man, she should never be greedy or take his money illegally.

A courtesan should form friendships with people who can introduce her to men, people who can help her reverse her luck, acquire wealth and protect her from being bullied.

These people are:

> The police
> Lawyers
> Astrologers
> Powerful men
> Educated men
> Teachers
> Confidants
> Businessmen
> Merchants

Some men may be associated with simply for getting their money, such as men who have independent income or are conceited or boast too much. Men who possess excellent qualities should be turned to for the sake of love and fame.

The good qualities of a man are:

Educated
Worldly wise
Sense of propriety
Artistic, verbal
High energy
Far-seeing
Intelligent
Persevering
Devoted
Happy, good-natured
Liberal
Affectionate to his parents
Sociable
Athletic
Healthy and strong
Not addicted to drink or drugs
Lusty, lovable
Independent means of livelihood
Free from envy and suspicion

The good qualities of a woman are:

Attractive
Amiable
Admires good qualities in others
Admires fine things
Enjoys wealth
Lusty
Firm minded
An equal sexual partner
A willing student
Not greedy
Sociable
Artistic
Intelligent
Good disposition
Good manners
Straightforward

Grateful

Considers her moves, plans and actions

Active

Consistent

A sense of propriety

Speaks kindly

Laughs softly

Not a gossip

Doesn't speak with anger, greed, stupidity

Skilled in the arts of the Kama Sutra

The following are the types of men that should be avoided by courtesans or any woman:

Sickly

One with body odor or bad breath

One whose wife is dear to him

Speaks harshly

Suspicious

Greedy

Shows no mercy or pity

A thief

Conceited

Disrespectful

One who can be bought

Extremely bashful

Vatsyayana believes that courtesans turn to men because they want wealth, freedom from problems and love. A courtesan should not sacrifice money for love, because money is her goal. However, even if she is invited to have intercourse, she should not at once consent. She should first determine if the man is to her liking by sharing time and conversation with him. If she likes him, she can proceed. She can enhance the relationship by doing things he enjoys, by giving him small gifts or by consulting him about business.

When a lover comes to her home, a courtesan should feed him, surround him with flowers and give him colognes and fragrant oils. She should demonstrate her artistic and conversational skills. She should give him loving, affectionate gifts and exchange some of her things for his. She should delight him with her skill in sexual enjoyment and apply it tenderly. ❦

The extent of the love of women is not known,
even by the men they love.

It is a subtle, natural intelligence in all women.
Though they love men,
become indifferent towards them,
give them delight,
abandon them or take all their money,
women are hardly ever known in their true light.

Chapter Two

Living Like a Wife

"When a courtesan is living as a wife with her lover, she should behave like a chaste woman and do everything to his satisfaction." Vatsyayana

A woman can win a man's favor by:

Expressing wonder at his knowledge and sexual prowess
Being open and willing to learn the Kama Sutra from him
Remember and practice the ways he teaches her to please him sexually
Keeping his secrets
Telling him her desires and secrets
Concealing her anger
Never neglecting him in bed
Touching him in his favorite places
Kissing and embracing him while he's sleeping
Looking at him anxiously when he's distracted
Showing neither shamelessness or bashfulness
Hating his enemies
Loving those who are dear to him
Showing a liking for what he likes
Matching his spirits, high or low
Not prolonging anger
Showing her love in deeds, signs and hints, not words
Remaining silent while he's sleeping, drunk or sick
Listening attentively
Praising him
Replying with wit
Worrying over him when he sighs, yawns, sneezes or falls down
Wearing his gifts

Consoling him when he's sick, in pain, dispirited or unfortunate
Expressing a desire not to live without him
Dressing with care each day
Not acting too freely with him
Placing his hands on her loins, bosom and forehead and falling asleep after feeling the pleasure of his touch
Sitting on his lap and falling asleep there
Wishing to have his child
Desiring not to live longer than he does
Respecting his religious vows and customs
Making no distinction between her wealth and his
Not going out too often without him
Accompanying him when he wants her to
Taking delight in using things he's used
Eating his left-over food
Venerating his family, his disposition, artistic skill, learning, complexion, native country, friends, good qualities, age, sweet temper
Asking him to sing or perform as he is able
Going to him regardless of fear, cold, heat, rain
Saying that even in the next life they will be lovers
Adapting her tastes, disposition and actions to his liking

When a man sets off on a trip, the woman should make him swear he will return quickly. When the man returns home, she should rejoice.

A man is attached to a woman when they share the same goals, when he trusts her and is indifferent to money in her regard.

The extent of the love of women is not known, even by the men they love. It is a subtle, natural intelligence in all women. Though they love men, become indifferent towards them, give them delight, abandon them or take all their money, women are hardly ever known in their true light. ❧

Chapter Three

Getting Money; Changes in a Lover's Feelings; Ways to Get Rid of a Man

"Money is got out of a lover in two ways: by natural or lawful means, and by artifices." Vatsyayana

When women use intrigue to get money from men, they always double their money. The schemes used for getting money from a lover are:

Taking money for purchases and not buying them or buying them for less
Praising his intelligence to his face
Pretending to be obligated to make charitable gifts
Pretending her valuables have been stolen, destroyed by fire or broken by her housekeepers
Using other people to tell him how much money she spent traveling to see him
Contracting debts for his sake
Refusing to visit friends because of not having the money to give them gifts
Engaging artists to do something for her lover
Having to pay expenses for friends
Pretending to be ill and charging the cost of her treatment
Helping a friend
Selling her belongings to give him a gift
Needing to buy more impressive household goods
Informing him that other women make more money than she
Embellishing the gains of other women

A woman should always know the state of mind and feelings of her lover from the changes in his disposition. The behavior of a lover who is losing interest is recognized by the following signs:

He gives her less than she wants or something altogether different
He bolsters her hopes with promises
He does not fulfill her desires
He forgets his promises
He sleeps at a friend's house under some pretense
He speaks to friends of a former lover

When a woman finds her lover's disposition changing, she should take possession of all his best things before he becomes aware of it. If her lover is wealthy and has always treated her well, she should treat him with respect. If he is poor and destitute, she should get rid of him as if she never even knew him.

The means of getting rid of a lover are as follows:

Describing his habits and vices as disagreeable
Speaking about a subject of which he knows nothing
Showing no admiration for his learning
Putting down his pride
Seeking the company of more intelligent men
Disregarding him
Condemning men who share her lover's faults
Not giving him her mouth to kiss
Refusing access to the lower parts of her body
Disliking love ornaments made by his nails and teeth
Keeping still during intercourse
Wanting him to make love when he's tired
Laughing at his attachment to her
Not responding to his embraces
Pretending to be sleepy
Going out when she knows he wants to be with her
Misconstruing his words
Laughing for no reason
Not paying attention
Interrupting him with her own stories
Reciting his faults and vices and declaring them incurable
Using words that cut him to the quick
Not looking at him when he approaches her
Asking him the impossible
Finally, dismissing him ✤

Chapter Four

Reunion With a Former Lover

"When a courtesan abandons her present lover after all his wealth is exhausted, she may then consider about her reunion with a former lover" Vatsyayana

A courtesan should return to a former lover if he is still attracted to her and only if he is wealthy. However, there are other considerations, especially if he is living with another woman. If the man has left several women, she should not approach him because he might be fickle and indifferent to the qualities of women. If he was driven away by one woman because she could make better money with another man, he is a good choice because he might be more generous with a new woman to spite the old one. If he has been driven away because he is stingy, he is not a good option for any woman. A former lover should be accepted back only if he gives her plenty of money before they get back together. When a woman wants an old lover back, she should find out why he left her in the first place. If he left her because she was lacking something and he didn't find it in another woman, she might take him back if he still has affection for her, and especially if he is willing to pay her money for his bad behavior.

Before a lover is accepted back, the woman should consider the following:

> Does he still have affection for her?
> Is he willing to spend lots of money on her?
> Was he unable to find her fine qualities in another woman?
> Is he coming back for revenge because she didn't satisfy him sexually?
> Is he returning only to collect the money he spent on her?
> Is he coming back to demoralize her?
> Is he coming back to steal her from her present lover, then leave her

If, after considering all these things, she is sure he is pure and honest, she

89

can take him back. If his intentions are not good, avoid him.

If a former lover was driven away from one woman and has resorted to a second woman, the courtesan should try to win him after considering the following things:

Was he driven away for no good reason?
Would he come back if she just had a chance to speak to him again?
Would it hurt the pride of her present lover?
Has he become wealthy? Or been promoted?
Is he separated from his wife?
Will taking him back clear the way to a richer lover?
Is he now independent?
Does he live apart from his family?
Since his wife no longer respects him, can he be separated from her?
Should she discredit him by getting him back and prove how fickle he is?

When a courtesan takes up with a former lover, she should convince him that she hates her present lover. She should speak to him only of her love for him and fondly recall the love ornaments he gave her. These love ornaments should symbolize a specific kind of lovemaking, such as his way of kissing her.

When a woman has to choose between two lovers, one of whom is a stranger, she might choose the lover she knows well because she can easily please and satisfy him. However, a former lover who has spent all his money might still not be able or willing to give her much money. He might not be as reliable as the new lover.

The courtesan might take back a former lover just long enough to destroy his relationship with a woman she dislikes. A reunion with a former lover can happen in order to have a certain effect on a present lover; such as to make him jealous or pay more attention to her. When a man is overly attached to a woman and he is afraid of losing her, he will overlook her faults and give her more money.

A courtesan should be agreeable to the man who is attached to her and despise the man who does not care for her. If, while she is living with one man, a messenger from another man comes, she might refuse to listen to his negotiations or arrange a time for the man to visit her. However, she should not leave a current lover who may be attached to her. ❧

A wise woman should only
renew her connection with a former lover
if she is satisfied that good fortune,
love and friendship are likely to result.

Chapter Five

Ways of Making Money

"When a courtesan is able to realize much money every day, by reason of many customers, she should not confine herself to a single lover." Vatsyayana

When a courtesan has many customers, she should establish her rate for one night. She should consider the location, season and condition of the people. She should take into consideration her good looks and fine qualities, and compare her rates with other courtesans. She can then inform her lovers, friends and acquaintances of these charges. If, however, she can earn a great income from a single lover, she may stay with him as a wife.

When a courtesan has the chance of equal gain from two men, she might give preference to the one who gives her money, not goods or gifts. With money she can always buy things she needs and likes.

When the same effort is required to win any two lovers who offer equal things in return, a choice between them might be aided by a friend. The courtesan should also look to their personal qualities or luck.

When one lover is attached and the other is simply generous, choose the one who is attached because he can be induced to be generous. A man who is simply generous cannot be made love to with real attachment. Among those who are attached to her, a rich man should always be preferred to a poor one.

When one lover is generous and another is ready to do a service for the courtesan, the latter might be preferred. However, a man who does a service could feel he has earned the woman's obligation. A generous man does not care for what he has given. Her choice should be guided by the likelihood of her own future gain.

When one of the two lovers is grateful and the other liberal, the liberal one might be preferred. However, liberal men are generally arrogant, plain spoken, inconsiderate and will leave the courtesan abruptly, even if what they have been told about her is lies. The generous man, on the other hand, might not leave abruptly because he knows the pains she has taken to please him.

When there is a choice between the request of a friend and the chance for making money, the money-making proposition might be preferred. Vatsyayana believes that money can be obtained tomorrow as well as today, but if the request of a friend is ignored, he might become alienated. If the courtesan pretends a prior commitment to her friend, then she still might be able to take advantage of the money-making proposition.

When the chance of getting money and the chance of avoiding some disaster come at the same time, getting money should be preferred. However, money has only a limited importance, and a disaster once averted might never occur again. The size of the disaster should impact the choice.

Money should be spent as follows:

> In charitable works
> Clothing
> Food and drink
> Jewelry

A courtesan should only accept a small amount of money when:

> She wants to keep a particular man from some other woman
> She wishes to separate a man from a particular woman
> To deprive another woman of making money with a man
> If she thinks it would increase her luck or fortune
> If she thinks it would make her more appealing to all men
> If she needs a man's help
> If she is really attached to a man and loves him
> If it is to return a favor from him
> If her only motive is desire

A courtesan should get as much money as possible from a man when:

> A lover intends to abandon her for another
> When she thinks her lover is about to return to his wife
> When he's squandered all his money
> When he gets fired from his job
> When he is fickle

A courtesan should look to her future welfare and live like a wife with a man when:

> Her lover is about to receive valuable gifts
> He attains a position of authority
> Is about to inherit a fortune
> When he makes money in stocks or commodities
> When nothing done for him is done in vain
> When he is always true to his word

In considering her present and future income, a courtesan should avoid people who have struggled to make a living, and those who have become selfish and hard-hearted. She should try to align herself with prosperous people. She should become acquainted with energetic and liberal-minded men who, even for some small thing, would be pleased to give her a large sum of money. ❦

An ancient verse says
"Men want pleasure and women want money"
so women should study
this part of the Kama Sutra particularly.

Chapter Six

Gains and Losses

"It sometimes happens that while gains are being sought for, or expected to be realized, losses only are the result of our efforts." Vatsyayana

*T*he causes of these losses are:

Weak intellect
Excessive love, pride, conceit, simplicity, confidence, anger
Carelessness
Recklessness
Influence of wrong advice
Accidental circumstances

The results of these losses are:

Expenses
Destruction of future good fortune
Halting of expected gains
Sour disposition
Unfriendly toward others
Loss of health and hair
Accidents

There are three kinds of gains and losses: wealth (Artha), religious merit (Dharma) and pleasure (Kama).

Consequential gains are gains that come along while others are sought.
Simple doubt happens when gain is uncertain.
Mixed doubts result when either of two things happen or not.

When one thing is done and two results take place, it is called a combination of results.

If several results follow from the same action, it is called a combination of results on every side.

For example, if a courtesan living with a great man acquires wealth and also meets other people who can increase her fortune, she has consequential gain. When a courtesan living with a man simply gets money, this is called a gain of wealth with no other gain. When a courtesan receives money from people other than her lover, she might ruin her reputation and gain from her present lover. This is called a gain of wealth accompanied by losses. When a courtesan goes to her own expense to divert a threat to great gain, she looses money but might gain some future fortune. When a courtesan is kind to stingy, bragging, ungrateful men and gets no benefit, she does not gain anything.

There are three kinds of doubts:

Doubts about wealth
> When a courtesan doubts how much a man may give or spend.
> When a courtesan has been uncivil to a man and might lose money because of it.

Doubts about religious merit
> When a courtesan feels doubtful about whether she is right to abandon a lover whose money she has exhausted.
> When a courtesan feels doubtful about abandoning a current lover.

Doubts about pleasures
> When a courtesan cannot get a lover to her liking.

Doubt about the loss of pleasure
> When a courtesan speaks up and reveals her love, then is concerned that she might not get her heart's desire, this is called a doubt about the loss of pleasure.

Mixed Doubts
> These may come from intercourse with a stranger or an authority figure and may or may not be productive.

Gain or Loss of Pleasure

Depending on the man, a courtesan may gain or lose pleasure when she relies only on gossip about him but goes to him anyway.

If a courtesan gets both wealth and pleasure from living with a lover, it is called a gain on both sides. When a courtesan lives with a lover at her own expense and he takes money he previously gave her, it is called a loss on both sides. When a courtesan is unsure whether a new lover could become attached or whether he could give her anything, it is called a doubt on both sides about gain.

When she is uncertain whether a former enemy is won over with her own money and might still injure her, hold a grudge or steal from her, this is called a doubt on both sides about loss. A gain on both sides happens when a courtesan gets money from a man she may go to see and also from one she did not go to see. A loss on both side happens when a courtesan has to risk further expense if she goes to see a man, and then risks an irremediable loss if she does not go to see him.

When a courtesan is uncertain whether a particular man would give her anything without incurring expense, or whether neglecting him would yield something, this is called a doubt on both sides about gain.

When a courtesan wonders whether an old enemy will take her back or steal from her, or whether going back to him might court disaster, this is called a doubt on both sides about loss.

A courtesan should act so as to acquire gain and to ward off disaster. Men should give her money and pleasure, and grant her particular desires. She should be conscious of what she can accomplish through a man.

An ancient verse says, "Men want pleasure and women want money," so women should study this part of the Kama Sutra particularly. ❧

PART SEVEN

ATTRACTING OTHERS

Chapter One

Personal Adornment; Conquering Hearts; Tonics and Aphrodisiacs

"When a person fails to obtain the object of his desires by any of the ways previously related, he should then have recourse to other ways of attracting others to himself. If the bone of a peacock or of a hyena be covered with gold, and tied on the right hand, it makes a man lovely in the eyes of other people." Vatsyayana

Personal Adornment

Appealing looks and good qualities are the most natural means of making people attractive to each other. In the absence of these, a man or a woman can resort to artificial means, or to art. The following ideas may be useful.

Rouge, powder, blushers, liquid foundation, eyebrow pencil, eye shadow and lipstick can be used to adorn the face. Black mascara, when applied to the eyelashes, has the effect of making a person look lovely. A dye made from the henna plant can be used to make temporary but lovely designs to adorn the hands, body and fingernails. Using henna to color dark hair produces lustrous reddish highlights and covers graying hair.

Many natural products can be used to alter and improve the appearance of the skin. Use elder flower water as a toner for dry skin. Lotions containing black walnut bark darken the skin and give the appearance of a suntan. Egg whites or honey applied to the skin tighten the pores. Lotions containing bitter orange blossoms help make dry skin look lustrous and younger. Lavender water reduces puffiness, helps acne and balances oily skin. Leaves and flowers of the cowslip reduce wrinkles.

Make breath alluringly sweet by using citrus, cloves, fennel, peppermint, strawberry, rosemary powder or thyme, and by eating fresh apples.

Men and women can use colognes, perfumes and lotions to make the skin fragrant and appealing. A cologne containing the essence of the blue lotus flower is thought to be particularly appealing on a man.

A woman might enhance her loveliness by remaining aloof. Men often ardently desire a woman because she makes herself scarce or difficult to approach. She should only make herself available to a man who can bring her wealth and happiness.

Conquering Hearts

When a daughter arrives at puberty, her mother should introduce her to young men who are her equals in age, disposition and education. The mother should shelter her daughter and only encourage relationships that will be advantageous to her and her family.

The daughter can attract and win successful young men by meeting them at school, at concerts or at the homes of friends. She should be allowed to have a relationship with the young man who is most appealing to her.

Tonic Medicines

Editor's note: Aphrodisiac use should first be researched by studying medicine, herbology or used on the recommendation of confidential relatives or friends. Try nothing whose effects are doubtful, impure, injurious to the body or are made from animal products. Use only wholesome, safe, healthy things approved by reliable sources.

Vatsyayana believes that certain natural ingredients rubbed on a man's penis can make a woman subject to his will. These two lists may have had some value more than 1500 years ago and they are included for their curiosity value:

white thorn apple
long pepper
honey
camel bones
hawk bones
peacock bones
vulture bones
funeral flowers
red arsenic
sulfur
monkey excrement

mango oil
ghee
red onions
sesame seeds
sparrow eggs
wheat flour and beans
milk and sugar mixture
ghee
fennel
asparagus
barley

To increase sexual vigor, Vatsyayana recommends milk mixed with sugar or licorice. Even today, people believe that certain herbs and foods can act as aphrodisiacs; things such as:

ambergris
anemone
cactus flowers
celery
cloves
cyclamen
damiana
fo-ti-tieng
galanga
ginger
ginseng
guarana
jasmine
juniper tea
kava kava
mandrake
a meat diet
musk
parsley
periwinkle
saw palmetto
valerian
yohimbe
Viagra ❀

Chapter Two

Ways to Excite Desire

"If a man is unable to satisfy a Hastini, or Elephant woman, he should have recourse to various means to excite her passion. At the commencement he should rub her yoni with his hand or fingers and not begin to have intercourse with her until she becomes excited, or experiences pleasure. This is one way of exciting a woman." Vatsyayana

Men can also use devices that are put around the penis to supplement its length or thickness to fit the woman's vaginal opening. These things should be soft, cool, provocative and made to the couple's liking.

All penis rings should be of the same size as the penis. Some of the following types can be used:

    Rings with a textured outer surface
    A "couple" is two rings used together
    The "bracelet" is made by joining three or more rings until they match the length of the penis
    A "single bracelet" can be formed by wrapping a single wire around the penis

    A dildo, softened with lotions or oils, can be tied on the man.

Certain lotions or ointments rubbed on the penis can cause a numbing or tingling sensation which is said to increase the couple's pleasure by delaying the man's orgasm.

Certain plant and herbal mixtures are said to increase sexual pleasure. Civet, used in a bath, is said to be an aphrodisiac. Gilly flower condiment, juniper tea, valerian, maidenhair fern, musk and parsley are said to increase sexual pleasure.

Certain ointments and creams can lubricate the vaginal opening to make intercourse easy and more pleasurable.

Some shampoos and lotions can be used to make the hair more appealing. They can lighten, darken or change the color. Some help slow down hair loss.

Lipstick can be used to color the lips or make them moist and appealing.

Certain herbs and foods can cause intoxication, change the color of other foods and liquids, or restore and preserve health.

The man and woman who pay attention to the true principles of the science of love are not driven solely by desire. Acts should never be indulged in purely for the sake of science.

The Kama Sutra was composed for the benefit of the world by Vatsyayana, a contemplator and student of religion. This work is not intended to be used merely as an instrument for satisfying desires. By respecting others and not becoming a slave to his passions, an intelligent, cautious person finds success in everything he undertakes. ❧

"Woman is fire, O Guatama,
her haunch, the fuel;
the hairs on her body, the smoke;
the yoni, the flame;
intercourse, the coals;
the fits of enjoyment, the sparks.

The gods offer seed in this fire.
From this offering man springs forth."

BRHADARANYAKA UPANISHAD

PART EIGHT

THE ILLUSTRATED

POSITIONS

*I*ntroduction

*T*he desire to make love is deeply entwined in the fabric of all living things. For humans, it can be a playful skill, much like painting or creating music, which integrates numerous elements. A composition includes balance, texture, nuances of color and intensity, and variations on a given theme. Mastery is evidenced when the emotions of a receptive audience are touched and transformed. The same is true for the erotic arts.

According to the Kama Sutra, one woman or man can creatively entertain his or her lover with countless love-making positions and keep them as engaged as if they were frolicking with thirty-two different partners. Besides contributing to variety and creating exceptional episodes of delight, experimenting with different postures of love can also provide an atmosphere conducive to intimacy and bonding. Variety definitely adds zest to love making and, by keeping boredom out of the bedroom, enlivens and extends relationships.

In the words of the Kama Sutra, when a person avoids excesses and devotes equal attention to the major principles of life, consciousness opens up to success and peacefulness. The following illustrations of sexual postures are offered as inspiration and suggestion. In experimenting, let your criteria be what feels good to both of you. Find out what sparks your fire, be creative, have fun and include your heart. Follow one position, or all, and make up your own. Most of all—enjoy!

Embrace of the Jaghana

Lying together, face to face, the man presses the woman's jaghana, the area between her naval and thighs. She opens her legs to welcome him, crossing her feet at the ankles behind his back. The woman places one arm across his shoulders and the other under her left leg to softly caress his back. With his legs held closely together and supporting his upper body on his elbows, the man then mounts her to playfully bite, scratch or kiss her while making love.

Peircing Position

The man kneels facing the woman who lies on her back. She bends her legs at the knees drawing them close to her sides, thereby widening her vaginal opening. She rests the upper part of her body on her elbows. Caressing her breast with his right hand, the man uses his left hand to guide his penis. Once he is fully inserted, the woman presses her thighs together to increase the friction.

میرود چه غم است یه در بہ بند دجنا نکہ کتابید یہ کردل ازغمر برکند
شایدپہ درکشاید جنا کہ توان لبست یہ کو لبشوا زحیات دنیا ست

بود و در حجرہ ہم جلیس بر سم قدیم از در در آمد جنا نکہ نشاط ملاعیت

Yawing Position

The man kneels facing the woman who lies on her back. The woman bends her legs at the knees drawing them back, up and as far apart as possible. She then angles her left elbow to fully support her upper body. Her left arm reaches across her body to hold the right forearm of the man. Still kneeling, the man places his left hand above the woman's right ankle and right hand on her left foot—this helps her maintain the vagina's "yawning" position. When the man has fully inserted his penis, the woman uses the angle of her thighs to vary the depth of her lover's penetration. In a variation of this position, she straightens both of her legs and places them on her lover's shoulders.

114

یورپ میں بہت روشنی علم و ہنر ہے

حق یہ ہے کہ بے حیثمہ دیبوال ہے یہ ظلمات!

جن کے لہو کی طفیل آج بھی ہے اندلسی

خوش دل و گرم خلاط سادہ و روشن جبیں!

Twining Position

Semi-reclining the woman supports her upper body on her right elbow, her hand braced against the back of her head. Her left hand is held softly against the left side of her lover's chest. Kneeling, the man slides his right leg under the woman's legs, separating them and lifting her up between his legs. He embraces her with his right arm and holds her left breast gently in left his hand. The woman's left leg is wrapped around the man's back and she braces herself with her foot. Using this leg, she can press her body closer to his. Her right leg is bent at the knee and drawn back, allowing the man easier penetration. If the woman uses both legs to grip her lover's thighs to tighten her vagina, this is called the Pressing Position.

Rising Position

Reclining, the woman supports her upper body on her left elbow. Her right arm is placed across the shoulders of her lover, her hand grasping his right shoulder. Her legs are open and upright and spread wide to accommodate her lover's body. Her left leg crosses over her right knee behind his back. Kneeling, the man clasps the woman to him with his right arm. Gently holding her left forearm in his right hand, he penetrates her deeply. He kisses her on the right side of her face, close to her ear.

یورپ میں بہت روشنی علم و ہنر ہے
حق یہ ہے کہ بے چشمہ حیواں ہے یہ ظلمات!

جن کے لہو کی طفیل آج بھی ہے اندلسی
خوش دل و گرم اختلاط سادہ و روشن جبیں!

Crab's Position

Lying flat on her back, the woman bends both legs at the knees and draws them up together until they press against her stomach. Her left arm is draped lightly across her lover's shoulders, her right arm is bent and the hand tucks under her face. She keeps her face turned from the man, making him yearn for her loving look. Kneeling in front of her and pressing into the back of her right thigh with his left forearm, he uses his hand to gently massage her right breast. His right arm supports his body as, like a crab, he crawls atop her and thrusts. Retracting her legs in this fashion tightens the vagina.

یورپ میں بہت روشنی علم و ہنر ہے
حق یہ ہے کہ بے چشمہ حیواں ہے یہ ظلمات!

جن کے لہو کی طفیل آج بھی ہے اندلسی
خوش دل و گرم ختلاط سادہ و روشن جبیں!

Widely Opened Position

Using pillows for support, the woman kneels and leans back until her bottom almost touches her heels. She then opens her knees and grips the man by his hips. The man moves up under the woman and supports her body. Since this position opens the vagina widely, the man can pierce it to its fullest extent.

The Top

Using cushions for support, the man reclines, tucking his knees under him. The woman squats and crawls toward him until he penetrates her fully. While his penis is still in her vagina, the woman moves and swivels her hips and knees first to one side, then the other. Vatsyayana believes that with a great deal of practice, the woman can eventually swivel her body completely around in a circle, like a top.

Sporting of a Sparrow

The man lies flat on his back, raises his knees and spreads them wide. His arms embrace the woman, who slowly crawls up the front of him. She braces her upper body by placing her right elbow on the cushion above the man's left shoulder. Her lower body is supported on her bent right knee. Pulling her left leg back as far as possible, she braces it with her left elbow. Though she keeps her arms and hands off her lover, she stares at him lovingly as she floats and dips like a sparrow above him.

Churning Position

Lying back, the man raises his legs. His arms are bent upwards, away from his lover. The woman squats in front of him and places her arms around his upraised legs to embrace him around his back. He then rests his legs on her knees. Inching forward, she allows him to penetrate her slowly and fully. Using her feet for leverage, she raises and lowers her vagina, never allowing his penis to be removed.

یورپ میں بہت روشنی علم و ہنر ہے
حق یہ ہے کہ بے چشمۂ حیواں ہے یہ ظلمات!

جن کے لہو کی طفیل آج بھی ہے اندلسی
خوش دلی و گرم خلط سادہ و روشن جبیں!

Turning Position

This position is accomplished in several stages. The lovers begin with the man supported by cushions and reclining with his knees tucked under. The woman lies atop, facing him, and allows him to penetrate her deeply. Careful to keep his penis completely inside her, she slowly reverses her body's position until she lies flat on her back against his stomach.

بودودر حجرہ ہم جلیس برسم قدیم ازدہ در آمد جنانکہ نشاط ملا عیت

Lotus Position

The man and woman sit upright imitating the yoga position called the lotus. Rising up on his feet and crouching over the woman, the man slowly raises his lover's legs to rest lightly on his thighs. She then raises her body up to meet his as he penetrates her. She rests her head on his chest and embraces him while he enfolds her body in his arms and nuzzles his face along the nape of her neck. This position works best when the woman's limbs are very flexible or she is an experienced student of yoga.

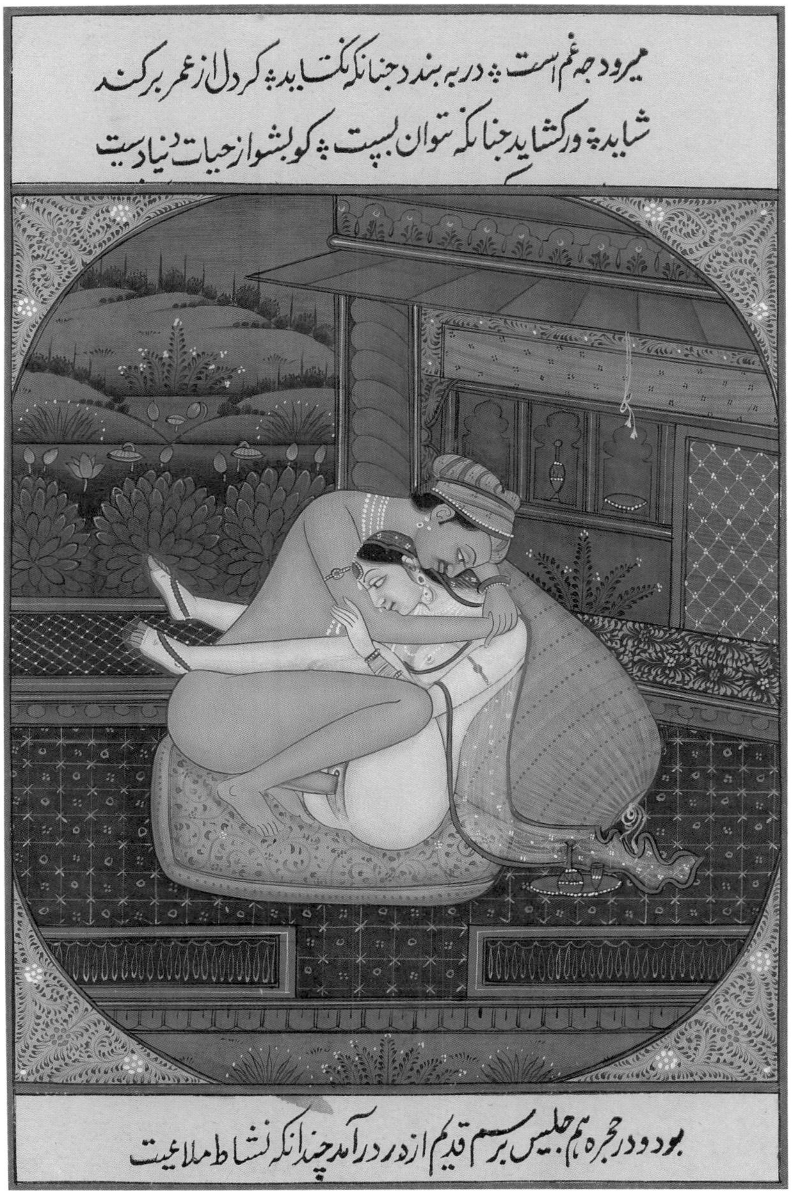

Wife of Indra

Both lovers are seated facing each other with their knees raised. The woman then lifts her feet above his knees. The man's left hand softly caresses the tender area under the woman's left arm, adjacent to her right breast. His right hand rests gently on her left shoulder. Though the woman's hands remain at her side, her eyes stroke the man with loving looks. With their legs spread so wide, the man's penis easily enters the woman's vagina. This position is named for the alluring and seductive wife of Indra, the Hindu god of rain and thunder.

Clasping Position

This position can be especially satisfying to the woman. She lies on her back and spreads her knees wide to more fully expose her clitoris. Her arms remain at her sides. Her lover faces her, bracing his hands on either side of her shoulders. Carefully and slowly, he penetrates her. If the woman slightly arches her back while in this position, she increases the friction between their bodies which will heighten and quicken her ultimate pleasure.

Splitting of the Bamboo

The woman lies on her back and raises her legs. Her left arm is bent up behind her head, the right hand clasped in her lover's. The man lies on the woman's left side and draws his knees up to meet her bottom. His right arm embraces her around the back and his left is under her raised right knee. His left hand clasps her right and he penetrates her. She then places one of her legs on her lover's elbow and the other along his back. She alternates these leg positions until they are both satisfied.

میرود جسم غم است پہ در یہ بند دجنانکہ یک شاید پہ کہ دل از غم بر کند
شاید پہ ورکشاید جنانکہ تو ان لبست پہ کولبسواز حیات دنیا دیست

بود و در حجرہ ہم جلیس بر سم قدیم از در در آمد جنانکہ نشاط ملائیت

Packed Position

Supported by cushions, the woman raises her knees. She places her left foot on the man's upper arm. Her left arm is held up and back while her right embraces her lover's shoulders and her left hand joins his. The man sits, crosses his feet and leans against the woman's right side. His left arm winds around her neck and his hand clasps hers. He caresses her lower leg as he penetrates her. The man then leans back and the woman crosses one of her thighs over the other. Now, she contracts her vagina to pack him tightly into her.

Sitting Position

The lovers are relaxed, facing each other. The woman spreads her legs back and wide. Using her left arm to brace her body, she drapes her right hand over the man's left shoulder. He sits up close to her body, bracing himself on his left hand and using his right to guide his penis.

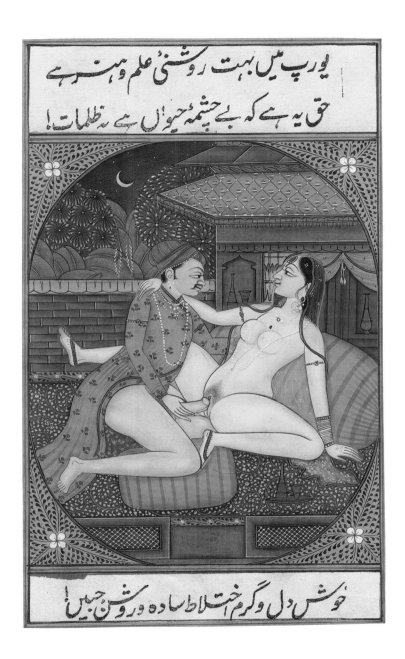

یورپ میں بہت روشنی علم و ہنر ہے
حق یہ ہے کہ بے چشمہ حیواں ہے یہ ظلمات!

خوش دل و گرم اختلاط سادہ و روشن جبیں!

The Peacock Position

The man squats on his heels and wraps his right arm around the woman. His left hand holds her right foot. The woman moves up his thighs and spreads her legs. She carefully places her left foot on the floor so that is provides balance and support for both of their bodies. Raising her right arm and spreading her right leg, she mounts her lover like a proud peacock. Using a bird-like fanning motion of her arm and leg, she can vary the pressure on his penis.

The Climbing Position

The man kneels in front of the woman and draws her towards him with his right arm. The woman wraps both arms around him. Lifting her body onto his erect penis, she straddles him, locking her ankles behind his back. The woman uses both her arms and legs to cling tightly to her lover. The sides of their faces press closely together just as their bodies join. When their bodies are both in position, the couple toasts its successful culmination. This position takes practice, strong muscles and good balance, especially on the part of the man.

یورپ میں بہت روشنی علم و ہنر ہے

حق یہ ہے کہ بے چشمہ حیواں ہے یہ ظلمات!

جن کے لہو کی طفیلی آج بھی ہے اندلسی

خوش دل و گرم اختلاط سادہ و روشن جبیں!

Supported Congress

This position requires a platform to support the woman. Sitting atop a stool or table, the woman raises her legs to an upright position and braces her ankles under the man's armpits. She wraps her arms around her lover's neck, clasping her hands. The man stands before her and uses his right hand to guide his penis into her vagina.

Suspended Congress

This position should be attempted only with the utmost care and only by those women who have limber, acrobatic talent. The woman bends completely backwards, places her hands on a cushion and raises her shoulders and head. Standing in front of the woman, the man raises his right leg and rests it gently on the woman's shoulders. His right arm is slipped under his right knee to stroke the woman's midriff while his left hand massages her left breast. He then penetrates her slowly and carefully.

*C*onclusion

*A*nd so the Kama Sutra of Vatsyayana draws to an end. The theme is the connection between men and women and their relationships with each other.

It is a work that should be studied by young and old. Young lovers will learn things they might not otherwise discover, or learn things before they make a mistake. Mature lovers will find real truths in it. The Kama Sutra can also be recommended to students of social science and humanity, and those devoted to history. The ideas presented here have filtered down through millenniums and continue to prove that human nature today is much the same as human nature long ago.

It has been said that Balzac, the French novelist, had an intuitiveness about the feelings of men and women and could describe them with an analysis worthy of a scientist. Vatsyayana must have had considerable knowledge of the humanities. His simple, true remarks have withstood the test of time and stand out as clear and valid today as when they were first written.

It must be remembered that in those early days there was apparently no idea of embellishing the work, either with a literary style, a flow of language, or verbose writing. The author tells the world what he knows in very concise language, without any attempt to produce an interesting story. From his facts, how many novels could be written! Indeed, the Kama Sutra has formed the basis of many stories and tales of past centuries.

Some curious recipes have been mentioned. Many of them are as ancient as the Kama Sutra itself. Sir Richard Burton points out that in later similar works these recipes and prescriptions appear to have increased both in quality and quantity. They cover a variety of topics, including:

Hastening the orgasm of the woman
Delaying the orgasm of the man
Aphrodisiacs
Thickening and enlarging the penis
Rendering it sound and strong, hard and lusty
Narrowing and contracting the vaginal opening
Perfuming the vaginal track
Removing and destroying body hair
Purifying the womb
Causing pregnancy
Preventing miscarriage
Ensuring easy labor
Birth control
Thickening and beautifying the hair
Obtaining a good black color to it
Whitening and bleaching it
Conditioning it
Clearing acne
Removing skin discoloration
Enlarging a woman's breasts
Uplifting pendulous breasts
Giving fragrance to the skin
Removing perspiration odors
Moisturizing the body after bathing
Sweetening the breath
Drugs and charms for fascinating, overcoming, and subduing men or women
Recipes enabling a woman to attract and preserve her husband's love
Magical eye lotions to win love and friendship
Prescriptions for making another person submissive
Pills and charms
Fascinating incense
Magical verses which have the power of fascination

Of the recipes given, many are absurd. But then again, so are some used now. Love potions, charms and herbal remedies have been used since ancient times and some people still believe in them.

And now, a few words about the author of the work, the good old sage Vatsyayana. Unfortunately, virtually nothing can be discovered about his life, his belongings or his surroundings. He states that he wrote the work while leading the life of a contemplator and religious student, probably in Benares in India. Throughout the Kama Sutra he gives us the benefit of his experience and opinions. These bear the stamp of age, not youth. This work could hardly have been written by a young man. The Kama Sutra remains a bright and guiding star to succeeding generations, a lasting treasure.

" In the embrace of his beloved,
a man forgets the whole world—
everything both within and without.

In the same way,
he who embraces the Self,
knows neither within
nor without."

UPANISHAD